DORLING KINDERSLEY **DK** EYEWITNESS GUIDES

WORLD WAR I

Early British
reconnaissance
aircraft

Signboard from
Ypres station, 1916

Book that stopped a bullet

Early gas helmet

British "carcass"
incendiary bomb

British 20 lb (9 kg)
Hales bomb

French tin soldiers

German incendiary
bomb, dropped
during first air
raid on London

Model of British motor ambulance
used on the Western Front

Prussian Iron
Cross

DK EYEWITNESS GUIDES

WORLD WAR I

US Distinguished
Service Cross

Written by
SIMON ADAMS

Photographed by
ANDY CRAWFORD

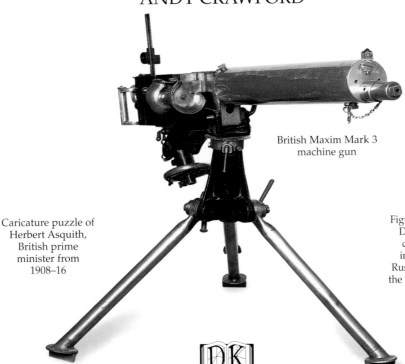

British Maxim Mark 3
machine gun

Caricature puzzle of
Herbert Asquith,
British prime
minister from
1908–16

Figurine of Grand
Duke Nicolas,
commander-
in-chief of the
Russian armies at
the start of the war

DK

A Dorling Kindersley Book

IN ASSOCIATION WITH
THE IMPERIAL WAR MUSEUM

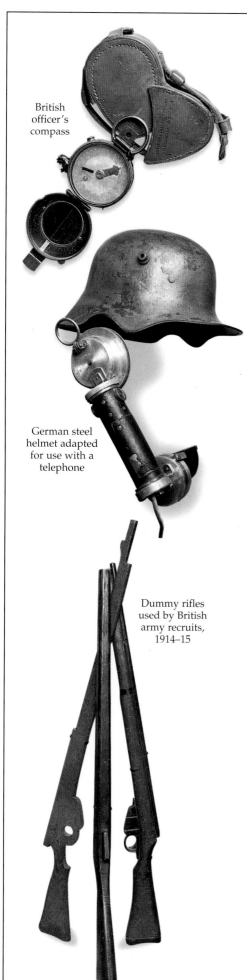

British officer's compass

German steel helmet adapted for use with a telephone

Dummy rifles used by British army recruits, 1914–15

Dorling Kindersley

LONDON, NEW YORK, SYDNEY, DELHI, PARIS, MUNICH and JOHANNESBURG

Project editor Patricia Moss
Art editors Julia Harris, Rebecca Painter
Senior editor Monica Byles
Senior art editors Jane Tetzlaff, Clare Shedden
Category publisher Jayne Parsons
Managing art editor Jacquie Gulliver
Senior production controller Kate Oliver
Picture research Sean Hunter
DTP designers Justine Eaton, Matthew Ibbotson
Jacket designer Dean Price

This Eyewitness ® Guide has been conceived by Dorling Kindersley Limited and Editions Gallimard

First published in Great Britain in 2001 by Dorling Kindersley Limited 80 Strand, London WC2R 0RL

4 6 8 10 9 7 5 3

Copyright © 2001 Dorling Kindersley Limited, London

A CIP catalogue record for this book is available from the British Library.

ISBN 0-7513-30841

Colour reproduction by Colourscan, Singapore
Printed in China by Toppan Printing Co., (Shenzhen) Ltd

See our complete catalogue at

www.dk.com

French *Croix de Guerre* medal awarded for valour

British and German barbed wire

British steel helmet with visor

Grenade

German medical orderly's pouch

Contents

High
explosive
shells

Divided Europe

At the start of the 20th century, the countries of Europe were increasingly hostile to each other. Britain, France, and Germany competed for trade and influence overseas, while Austria-Hungary and Russia both tried to dominate the Balkan states of south-east Europe. Military tension between Germany and Austria-Hungary on the one hand and Russia and France on the other led to the formation of powerful military alliances. A naval arms race added to the tension. In 1912–13 two major wars broke out in the Balkans as rival states battled to divide Turkish-controlled lands between them. By 1914 the political situation in Europe was tense, but few believed that a continental war was inevitable.

HMS DREADNOUGHT
The launch of HMS *Dreadnought* in February 1906 marked a revolution in battleship design. With its 10 12-inch (30-cm) guns and a top speed of 21 knots, the British ship outperformed and outpaced every other battleship of the day. As a result, Germany, France, and other maritime nations began to design and build their own "Dreadnoughts", starting a worldwide naval armaments race.

KAISER WILHELM II
Wilhelm II became emperor of Germany in 1888, when he was just 29. He had a withered arm and other disabilities, but overcame them through his strong personality. As emperor, he tried to turn Germany from a European power to a world power, but his aggressive policies and arrogant behaviour upset other European nations, particularly Britain and France.

Some children had models of HMS Dreadnought and could recite every detail of her statistics

Hand-painted, tinplate toy battleship

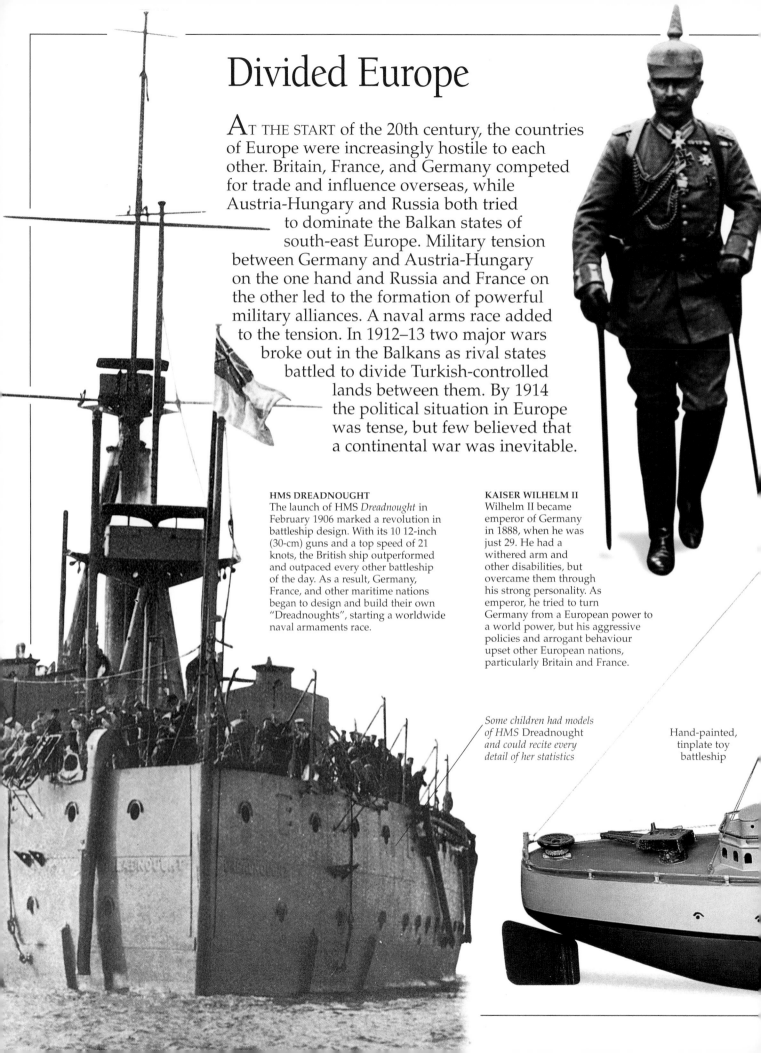

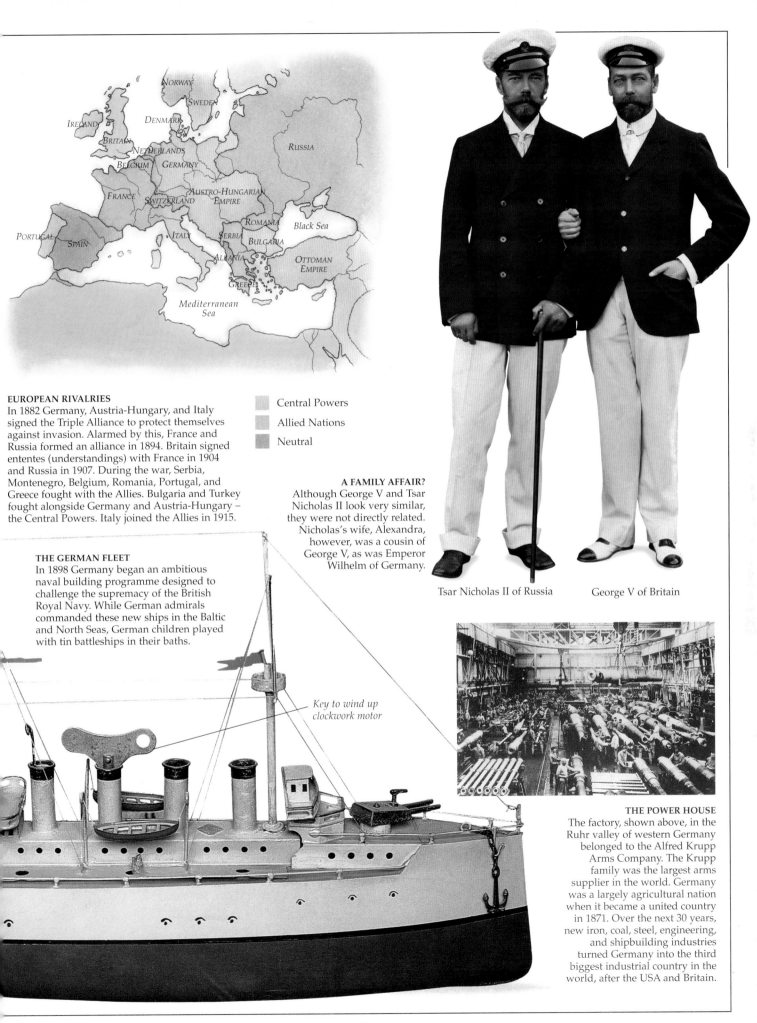

EUROPEAN RIVALRIES
In 1882 Germany, Austria-Hungary, and Italy signed the Triple Alliance to protect themselves against invasion. Alarmed by this, France and Russia formed an alliance in 1894. Britain signed ententes (understandings) with France in 1904 and Russia in 1907. During the war, Serbia, Montenegro, Belgium, Romania, Portugal, and Greece fought with the Allies. Bulgaria and Turkey fought alongside Germany and Austria-Hungary – the Central Powers. Italy joined the Allies in 1915.

Central Powers

Allied Nations

Neutral

A FAMILY AFFAIR?
Although George V and Tsar Nicholas II look very similar, they were not directly related. Nicholas's wife, Alexandra, however, was a cousin of George V, as was Emperor Wilhelm of Germany.

Tsar Nicholas II of Russia   George V of Britain

THE GERMAN FLEET
In 1898 Germany began an ambitious naval building programme designed to challenge the supremacy of the British Royal Navy. While German admirals commanded these new ships in the Baltic and North Seas, German children played with tin battleships in their baths.

Key to wind up clockwork motor

THE POWER HOUSE
The factory, shown above, in the Ruhr valley of western Germany belonged to the Alfred Krupp Arms Company. The Krupp family was the largest arms supplier in the world. Germany was a largely agricultural nation when it became a united country in 1871. Over the next 30 years, new iron, coal, steel, engineering, and shipbuilding industries turned Germany into the third biggest industrial country in the world, after the USA and Britain.

The fatal shot

On 28 JUNE 1914 the heir to the Austro-Hungarian throne, Archduke Franz Ferdinand, was assassinated in Sarajevo, Bosnia. Bosnia had been part of Austria-Hungary since 1908, but it was claimed by neighbouring Serbia. Austria-Hungary blamed Serbia for the assassination, and on 28 July declared war. What began as the third Balkan war rapidly turned into a European war. Russia supported Serbia, Germany supported Austria-Hungary, and France supported Russia. On 4 August, Germany invaded neutral Belgium on its way to France. It intended to knock France out of the war before turning its attention to Russia, thus avoiding war on two fronts. But Britain had guaranteed to defend Belgium's neutrality, and it too declared war on Germany. The Great War had begun.

THE AUSTRO-HUNGARIAN ARMY
The Austro-Hungarian empire had three armies – Austrian, Hungarian, and the "Common Army". Ten main languages were spoken! The official one was German, but officers had to learn their men's language, leading to frequent communication difficulties. The complex structure of the army reflected Austria-Hungary itself, which in reality was two separate monarchies ruled by one monarch.

MOBILIZE!
During July 1914, military notices were posted up across Europe informing citizens that their country's army was being mobilized (prepared) for war and that all those belonging to regular and reserve forces should report for duty.

GERMANY REJOICES
Germany prepared its army on 1 August, declaring war against Russia later the same evening and against France on 3 August. Most Germans in the cities were enthusiastic for the war and many civilians rushed to join the army in support of Kaiser and country. Germans in the countryside were less enthusiastic.

Austro-Hungarian *Reiter* (Trooper) of the 8th Uhlan (Lancer) Regiment

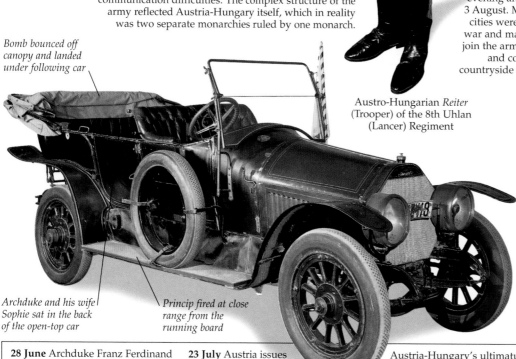

Bomb bounced off canopy and landed under following car

Archduke and his wife Sophie sat in the back of the open-top car

Princip fired at close range from the running board

ONE DAY IN SARAJEVO
The six assassins – five Serbs and one Bosnian Muslim – lay in wait along Archduke Ferdinand's route to the Austrian governor's residence in Sarajevo. One of them threw a bomb at Ferdinand's car, but it bounced off and exploded under the following car, injuring two army officers. The Archduke and his wife went to visit the injured officers in hospital 45 minutes later. When their car took a wrong turning, Gavrilo Princip stepped out of the crowd and shot the couple. Ferdinand's wife died instantly and he died 10 minutes later.

28 June Archduke Franz Ferdinand is assassinated in Sarajevo
5 July Germany gives its ally, Austria-Hungary total support for any action it takes against Serbia
23 July Austria issues a drastic ultimatum to Serbia, which would undermine Serbian independence
25 July Serbia agrees to most of Austria-Hungary's ultimatums, but still mobilizes as a safety precaution
28 July Austria-Hungary ignores Serbia's readiness to seek a peaceful end to the crisis and declares war
30 July Russia mobilizes in support of its ally, Serbia
31 July Germany demands that Russia stop its mobilization

German (above) and French (right) mobilization posters

VIVE LA FRANCE
The French army mobilized on 1 August. For many Frenchmen, the war was an opportunity to seek revenge for the German defeat of France in 1870–71 and the loss of Alsace-Lorraine to German control.

ALL ABOARD!
The German slogans on this westbound train read "Day trip to Paris" and "See you again on the Boulevard", as all Germans believed that their offensive against France would soon take them to Paris. French trains heading east towards Germany carried similar messages about Berlin.

"The lamps are going out all over Europe"

SIR EDWARD GREY
BRITISH FOREIGN SECRETARY, 1914

---

1 August Germany mobilizes against Russia and declares war; France mobilizes in support of its ally, Russia; Germany signs a treaty with Ottoman Turkey; Italy declares its neutrality
2 August Germany invades Luxembourg and demands the right to enter neutral Belgium, which is refused
3 August Germany declares war on France
4 August Germany invades Belgium on route to France; Britain enters the war to safeguard Belgian neutrality
6 August Austria-Hungary declares war on Russia
12 August France and Britain declare war on Austria-Hungary

War in the west

CHRISTMAS TREAT
The London Territorial Association sent each of their soldiers a Christmas pudding in 1914. Other soldiers received gifts in the name of Princess Mary, daughter of King George V.

Ever since the 1890s, Germany had feared that it would face a war on two fronts – against Russia in the east and against France, Russia's ally since 1893, in the west. Germany knew the chances of winning such a war were slim. By 1905, the chief of the German staff, Field Marshal Count Alfred von Schlieffen, had developed a bold plan to knock France swiftly out of any war before turning the full might of the German army against Russia. For this plan to work, the German army had to pass through Belgium, a neutral country. In August 1914, the plan went into operation. German troops crossed the Belgian border on 4 August, and by the end of the month, invaded northern France. The Schlieffen Plan then required the army to sweep around the north and west of Paris, but the German commander, General Moltke, modified the plan and instead headed east of Paris. This meant his right flank (side) was exposed to the French and British armies. At the Battle of the Marne on 5 September, the German advance was held and pushed back. By Christmas 1914, the two sides faced stalemate along a line from the Belgian coast in the north to the Swiss border in the south.

IN RETREAT
The Belgian army was too small and inexperienced to resist the invading German army. Here, soldiers with dog-drawn machine guns are withdrawing to Antwerp.

IN THE FIELD
The British Expeditionary Force (B.E.F.) had arrived in France by 22 August 1914. Its single cavalry division included members of the Royal Horse Artillery, whose L Battery fired this 13-pounder quick firing Mark I gun against the German 4th Cavalry Division at the Battle of Néry on 1 September. This held up the German advance into France for one morning. Three gunners in the battery received Victoria Crosses for their valour.

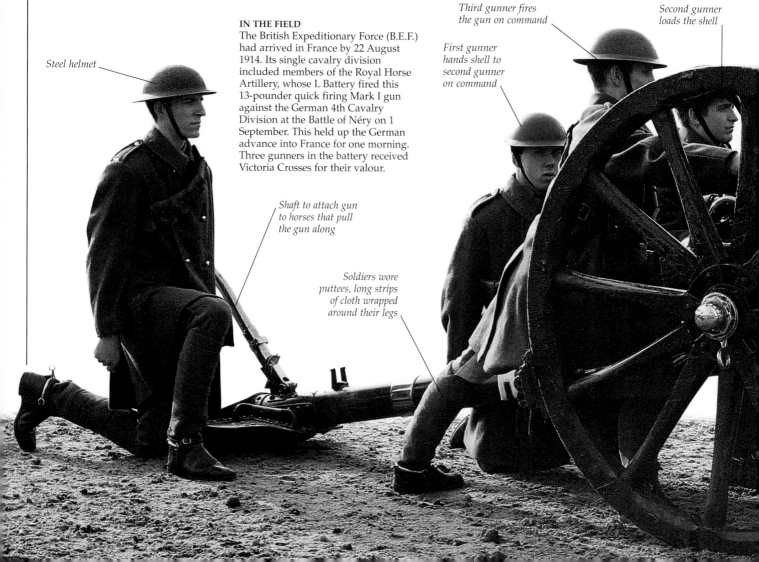

Third gunner fires the gun on command

Second gunner loads the shell

First gunner hands shell to second gunner on command

Steel helmet

Shaft to attach gun to horses that pull the gun along

Soldiers wore puttees, long strips of cloth wrapped around their legs

THE CHRISTMAS TRUCE

On Christmas Eve 1914, soldiers on both sides of the Western Front sang carols to each other in comradely greeting. The following day, troops along two-thirds of the front observed a truce. All firing stopped, and church services were held. A few soldiers crossed into no-man's-land to talk to their enemy and exchange simple gifts of cigarettes and other items. Opposite Ploegsteert Wood, south of Ypres, Belgium, a game of football took place between members of the German Royal Saxon Regiment and the Scottish Seaforth Highlanders. The Germans won 3–2. In some places, the truce lasted for almost a week. A year later, however, sentries on both sides were ordered to shoot anyone attempting a repeat performance.

Soldier shooting at enemy with a note saying "Christmas Eve – Get 'em!"

British and German soldiers greeting each other on Christmas Day

EYEWITNESS

Captain E.R.P. Berryman of the 2nd Battalion 39th Garwhal Rifles, wrote a letter home describing the truce. He told his family that the Germans had put up Christmas trees in their trenches. This cartoon illustrates the absurdity of his situation – shooting the enemy one day and greeting them as friends the next.

German trench

Rope wrapped around recoil mechanism

Fires 12.5 lb (5.6 kg) shells a distance of 5,395m (5,900 yards)

HEADING FOR THE FRONT

The German advance into northern France was so rapid that by early September, its troops were along the River Marne, only 40 km (25 miles) east of Paris. General Gallieni, military governor of Paris, took 600 taxis and used them to convey 6,000 men to the front line to reinforce the French 6th Army.

Fighting men

THE OUTBREAK OF WAR in Europe in August 1914 changed the lives of millions of men. Regular soldiers, older reservists, eager recruits, and unwilling conscripts all found themselves caught up in the war. Some of them were experienced soldiers, but many had barely held a rifle before. In addition to the European forces, both Britain and France drew heavily on armies recruited from their overseas colonies and from the British dominions. The design and detail of their uniforms differed considerably, although brighter colours soon gave way to khaki, dull blue, and grey.

France

Hat flaps could be pulled down to keep out the cold

Jerkin could be made of goat- or sheepskin

Ammunition pouch

GRAND DUKE NICOLAS
At the outbreak of war, the Russian army was led by Grand Duke Nicolas, uncle of Tsar Nicholas II. In August 1915, the Tsar dismissed his uncle and took command himself. As commander-in-chief, the Tsar dealt with the overall strategy of the war. The Russian armies were led by generals who directed the battles. The other warring countries employed similar chains of command.

Woollen puttees wrapped around shins

THE BRITISH ARMY
At the start of war, the British army contained 247,432 regulars and 218,280 reservists. Soldiers wore a khaki uniform consisting of a single-breasted tunic with a folding collar, trousers, puttees or leggings worn to protect the shins, and ankle-boots. In the winter soldiers were issued with additional items such as jerkins. Many wore knitted scarves and balaclavas sent from home.

Lee Enfield rifle No. 1 MkIII

British soldier

EMPIRE TROOPS
The British and French armies included large numbers of recruits from their colonial possessions in Africa, Asia, the Pacific, and the Caribbean. In addition, the British dominions of Australia, New Zealand, Canada, and South Africa sent their own armies to take part in the conflict. Many of these troops had never left their home countries before. These Annamites (Indo-Chinese), above, from French Indo-China were stationed with the French army at Salonika, Greece, in 1916. They wore their own uniforms rather than those of the French army.

EASTERN ALLIES
In Eastern Europe, Germany faced the vast Russian army, as well as smaller armies from Serbia and Montenegro. In the Far East, German colonies in China and the Pacific Ocean were invaded by Japan. These illustrations come from a poster showing Germany's enemies.

Thick boots to protect feet

Russia

France

Britain

Belgium

WESTERN ALLIES
In Western Europe, Britain, France, and Belgium were allied against Germany. The British and French armies were large, but the Belgian army was small and inexperienced. These illustrations come from a German poster identifying the enemy.

Steel helmets were issued in 1916

Field tunic (Waffenrock)

Tent cloth

Cartridge pouch

Mauser rifle

French infantrymen photographed in 1918

THE FRENCH ARMY
The French army was one of the largest in Europe. Including reservists and colonial troops, the French army totalled 3,680,000 trained men at the outbreak of war.

Water bottle

French infantryman, known as *le poilu*

Haversack with personal items

Stick grenade

Lebel rifle

Gas mask

THE GERMAN ARMY
The German army was the strongest in Europe because it had been preparing for war. At the outbreak of hostilities, it consisted of 840,000 men. All men under the age of 45 were trained for military service and belonged to the reserve army. On calling up the reserves, the German army could expand to over four million trained men.

German soldier

Russia

Serbia

Montenegro

Japan

Joining up

AT THE OUTBREAK OF WAR, every European country but one had a large standing army of conscripted troops ready to fight. The exception was Britain, which had a small army made up of volunteers. On 6 August 1914, the Secretary of War, Lord Kitchener, asked for 100,000 new recruits. Whole streets and villages of patriotic men queued to enlist. Most thought they would be home by Christmas. By the end of 1915, 2,446,719 men had volunteered, but more were needed to fill the depleted ranks of soldiers. In January 1916, conscription was introduced for all single men aged 18–41.

WAR LEADER
British Prime Minister Herbert Asquith was caricatured as "the last of the Romans" and replaced by David Lloyd George in December 1916.

THE TEST
Every British recruit had to undergo a medical test to make sure he was fit to fight. Large numbers failed this test, because of poor eyesight, chest complaints, or general ill health. Others were refused because they were under 19, although many lied about their age. Once he passed the test, the recruit took the oath of loyalty to the king and was then accepted into the army.

"YOUR COUNTRY NEEDS YOU"
A portrait of British War Minister, General Kitchener was used as a recruiting poster. By the time it appeared in late September 1914, however, most potential recruits had already volunteered.

Small box respirator gas mask

Haversack contained the filter of the small box respirator

Pouch contained three clips, which each held five bullets

Two sets of five ammunition pouches on belt

QUEUE HERE FOR KING AND COUNTRY
At the outbreak of war, long queues formed at recruiting offices around the country. Men from the same area or industry grouped together to form the famous Pals battalions, so they could fight together. By mid-September, half a million men had volunteered to fight.

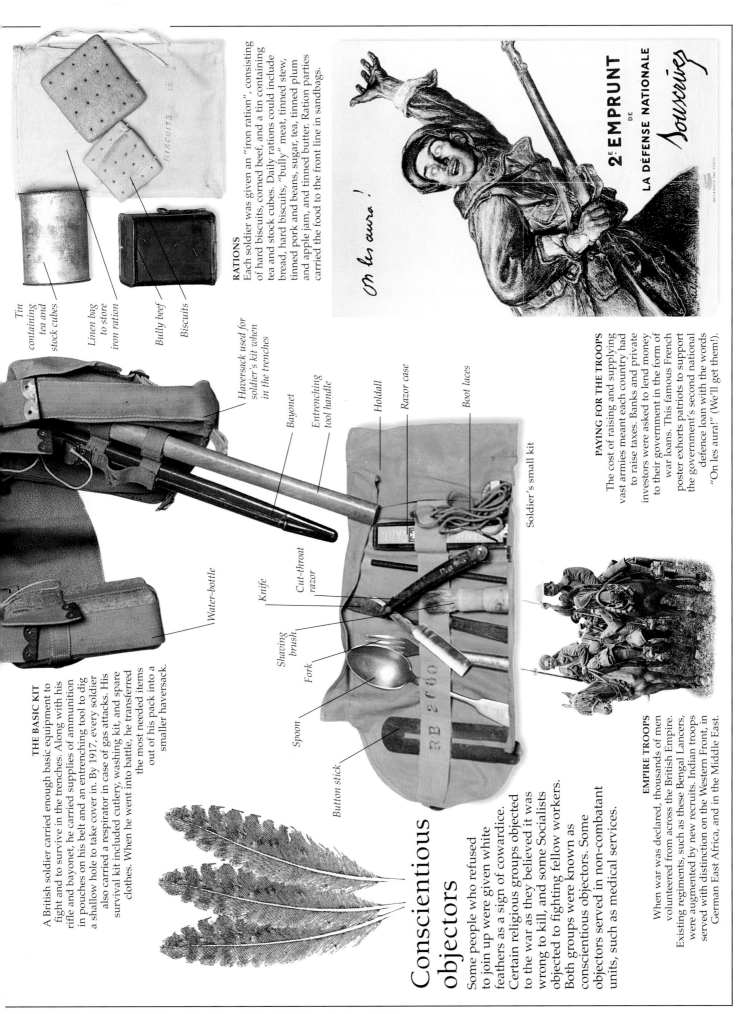

RATIONS

Each soldier was given an "iron ration", consisting of hard biscuits, corned beef, and a tin containing tea and stock cubes. Daily rations could include bread, hard biscuits, "bully" meat, tinned stew, tinned pork and beans, sugar, tea, tinned plum and apple jam, and tinned butter. Ration parties carried the food to the front line in sandbags.

Tin containing tea and stock cubes

Linen bag to store iron ration

Bully beef

Biscuits

On les aura!

2ᴇ EMPRUNT DE **LA DÉFENSE NATIONALE** *Souscrivez*

Haversack used for soldier's kit when in the trenches

Bayonet

Entrenching tool handle

Holdall

Razor case

Boot laces

Soldier's small kit

Water-bottle

Knife

Cut-throat razor

Shaving brush

Fork

Spoon

Button stick

THE BASIC KIT

A British soldier carried enough basic equipment to fight and to survive in the trenches. Along with his rifle and bayonet, he carried supplies of ammunition in pouches on his belt and an entrenching tool to dig a shallow hole to take cover in. By 1917, every soldier also carried a respirator in case of gas attacks. His survival kit included cutlery, washing kit, and spare clothes. When he went into battle, he transferred the most needed items out of his pack into a smaller haversack.

PAYING FOR THE TROOPS

The cost of raising and supplying vast armies meant each country had to raise taxes. Banks and private investors were asked to lend money to their government in the form of war loans. This famous French poster exhorts patriots to support the government's second national defence loan with the words "On les aura!" (We'll get them!).

EMPIRE TROOPS

When war was declared, thousands of men volunteered from across the British Empire. Existing regiments, such as these Bengal Lancers, were augmented by new recruits. Indian troops served with distinction on the Western Front, in German East Africa, and in the Middle East.

Conscientious objectors

Some people who refused to join up were given white feathers as a sign of cowardice. Certain religious groups objected to the war as they believed it was wrong to kill, and some Socialists objected to fighting fellow workers. Both groups were known as conscientious objectors. Some objectors served in non-combatant units, such as medical services.

Digging the trenches

AT THE OUTBREAK OF WAR, both sides on the Western Front expected to take part in massive military manoeuvres over hundreds of miles of territory, and to fight fast-moving battles of advance and retreat. No-one expected a static fight between two evenly matched sides. A stalemate occurred mainly because powerful long-range artillery weapons and rapid-fire machine guns made it dangerous for soldiers to fight in unprotected, open ground. The only way to survive such weapons was to dig defensive trenches.

Blade cover

━━━ Front line of trenches

THE FRONT LINE
By December 1914, a network of trenches stretched along the Western Front from the Belgian coast in the north down through eastern France to the Swiss border, 645 km (400 miles) in the south. By 1917, it was possible in theory to walk most of the length of the front along the winding trench network.

THE FIRST TRENCHES
Early trenches were just deep furrows, which provided minimal cover from enemy fire. These troops from the 2nd Scots Guards dug this trench near Ypres in October 1914. Their generals believed that such trenches were only temporary, as the "normal" war of movement would resume in the spring.

ENTRENCHING TOOLS
Each soldier carried an entrenching tool. With it, the soldier could dig a scrape – a basic protective trench – if he was caught out in the open by enemy fire. He could also use it to repair or improve a trench damaged by an enemy artillery bombardment.

American M1910 entrenching tool

SIGNPOSTS
Each trench was signposted to make sure no-one lost his way during an attack. Nicknames frequently became signposted names.

POSITIONING THE TRENCH
Neither side had great expertise in digging trenches at the outbreak of war, but they quickly learned from their mistakes. The Germans usually built trenches where they could best observe and fire at the enemy while remaining concealed. The British and French preferred to capture as much ground as possible before digging their trenches.

BOARDED UP
One of the main dangers of trench life was the possibility of being buried alive if the walls collapsed. By summer 1915, many German trenches were reinforced with wooden walls to prevent this happening. They were also dug very deep to help protect the men from artillery bombardments.

HOME SWEET HOME?
The Germans constructed very elaborate trenches because, as far as they were concerned, this was the new German border. Many trenches had shuttered windows and even doormats to wipe muddy boots on! Allied trenches were much more basic because the Allies expected to recapture the occupied territory.

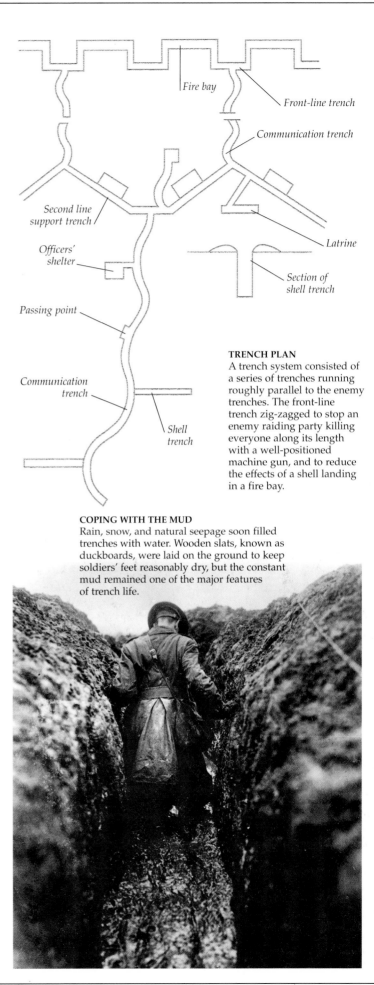

TRENCH PLAN
A trench system consisted of a series of trenches running roughly parallel to the enemy trenches. The front-line trench zig-zagged to stop an enemy raiding party killing everyone along its length with a well-positioned machine gun, and to reduce the effects of a shell landing in a fire bay.

COPING WITH THE MUD
Rain, snow, and natural seepage soon filled trenches with water. Wooden slats, known as duckboards, were laid on the ground to keep soldiers' feet reasonably dry, but the constant mud remained one of the major features of trench life.

Fire bay
Front-line trench
Communication trench
Second line support trench
Latrine
Officers' shelter
Section of shell trench
Passing point
Communication trench
Shell trench

Life in the trenches

DAYTIME IN THE TRENCHES alternated between short periods of intense fear, when the enemy fired, and longer periods of boredom. Most of the work was done at night when patrols were sent out to observe and raid enemy trenches, and to repair their own front-line parapets and other defences. Dawn and dusk were the most likely times for an enemy attack, so all the troops "stood to", that is manned the fire bays, at these times. The days were usually quiet, so the men tried to catch up on sleep while sentries watched the enemy trenches. Many soldiers used this time to write home or keep a diary of events. There were no set mealtimes on the front line, and soldiers ate as and when transport was available to bring food to the front by carrying parties. To relieve the boredom, soldiers spent one week to 10 days in the front line, then moved into the reserve lines, and finally went to a rear area to rest. Here, they were given a bath and freshly laundered clothes before returning to the trenches.

A LITTLE SHELTER
The trenches were usually very narrow and often exposed to the weather. The Canadian soldiers in this trench have built a makeshift canopy to shelter under. The sides are made of sandbags piled on top of each other.

Soldier removing mud from ammunition pouch with a piece of cloth

A RELAXING READ?
This re-creation from London's Imperial War Museum shows a soldier reading. While there was plenty of time for the soldiers to read during the day, they were often interrupted by rats scurrying past their feet and itching lice in their clothes.

CLEAN AND TIDY
The cleaning of kit and the waterproofing of boots was as much a part of life in the trenches as it was in the barracks back home. These Belgian soldiers cleaning their rifles knew that such tasks were essential to maintaining combat efficiency.

OFFICERS' DUG-OUT
This re-creation in London's Imperial War Museum of an officers' dug-out on the Somme in autumn 1916 shows the cramped conditions people endured in the trenches. The officer on the telephone is calling in artillery support for an imminent trench raid, while his weary comrade is asleep behind him on a camp bed. Official notices, photographs, and postcards from home are pinned around the walls.

French author Henri Barbusse (1873–1935) wrote of life in the trenches, denouncing the war in his novel *Le Feu* (*Under Fire*) of 1916.

Poem and self-portrait by British poet and artist Isaac Rosenberg (1890–1918)

The Menin Road (1918) by Paul Nash

Artists and poets

Some soldiers used their spare time in the trenches to write poems or make sketches. A huge number wrote long letters home, or kept a diary. After the war, many of these writings were published. Literary records of trench life made fascinating and shocking reading. In 1916, the British government began to send official war artists, such as Paul Nash (1889–1946), to the front to record the war in paint.

Paints and brushes belonging to British war artist Paul Nash

CAVE MEN
Ordinary soldiers – such as these members of the British Border Regiment at Thiepval Wood on the Somme in 1916 – spent their time off duty in "funk holes", holes carved out of the side of the trench, or under waterproof sheets. Unlike the Germans, the British did not intend to stay in the trenches too long, so did not want the soldiers to make themselves comfortable.

TRENCH CUISINE
These French officers are dining well in a reserve trench in a quiet area. Others were less fortunate, enduring tinned food or mass-produced meals cooked and brought up from behind the lines and reheated in the trench.

Soldiers served alongside a regiment of rats and lice

Ready to fight

It is easy to imagine that most of the action on the Western Front took place when soldiers left their trenches and fought each other in open ground, or no-man's-land, between the two opposing front lines. In reality, such events were far rarer than the constant battle between soldiers in their facing lines of trenches. Both armies took every opportunity to take shots at anyone foolish or unfortunate enough to be visible to the other side. Even soldiers trying to rescue wounded comrades from no-man's-land or retrieve bodies caught on the barbed-wire fences were considered fair targets. Raiding parties from one front line to the other added to the danger. This relentless war of attrition kept every soldier on full alert, and meant that a watch had to be kept on the enemy lines every hour of the day.

PREPARE TO FIRE
These German troops on the Marne in 1914 are firing through purpose-built gun holes. This enabled them to view and fire at the enemy without putting their heads above the parapet and exposing themselves to enemy fire. Later on in the war, sandbags replaced the earth ramparts. On their backs, the troops carry leather knapsacks with rolled-up greatcoats and tent cloths on top.

IN CLOSE QUARTERS
Soldiers were armed with a range of close-combat weapons when they went on raiding parties in case they needed to kill an enemy. The enemy could be killed silently so that the raiding soldiers did not draw attention to themselves. The weapons were rarely used.

French trench knife

German stick grenade

German club

German timed and fused ball grenade

British Mills bomb

WRITING HOME
Canon Cyril Lomax served in France in 1916–17 as a chaplain to the 8th Battalion Durham Light Infantry. As a non-combatant, he had time to describe in illustrated letters home some of the horrors he encountered. The armies of both sides had chaplains and other clergy at the front.

WALKING WOUNDED

This recreation in London's Imperial War Museum shows a wounded German prisoner being escorted by a medical orderly from the front line back through the trench system to a regimental aid post. Many, however, were not so fortunate. A soldier wounded in no-man's-land would be left until it was safe to bring him back to his trench, usually at nightfall. Many soldiers risked their lives to retrieve wounded comrades. Sadly some soldiers died because they could not be reached soon enough.

REGIMENTAL AID POST

Battalion medical officers, as shown in this recreation from London's Imperial War Museum, worked through the heat of battle and bombardment to treat the flood of casualties as best they could. They dressed wounds, tried to relieve pain, and prepared the badly wounded for the uncomfortable journey out of the trenches to the field hospital.

Path of bullet

SAVED BY A BOOK

The soldier carrying this book was lucky. By the time the bullet had passed through the pages, its passage was slowed enough to minimise the injury it caused.

ALWAYS IN ACTION

This photograph of Bulgarian soldiers was taken in 1915. It shows that soldiers could never let their guard down while in a trench. A permanent look-out must be kept, and guns always primed and ready in case the enemy mounted a sudden attack. The soldiers had to eat in shifts to ensure their constant readiness for battle.

"The German that I shot was a fine looking man ... I did feel sorry but it was my life or his"

BRITISH SOLDIER JACK SWEENEY, 21 NOVEMBER, 1916

Communication and supplies

COMMUNICATING WITH and supplying front-line troops is the biggest problem faced by every army. On the Western Front, this problem was particularly acute because of the length of the front line and the large number of soldiers fighting along it. In mid-1917, for example, the British army required 500,000 shells a day, and million-shell days were not uncommon. To supply such vast and hungry armies, both sides devoted great attention to lines of communication. The main form of transport remained the horse, but increasing use was made of mechanized vehicles. Germany made great use of railways to move men and supplies to the front. Both sides set up elaborate supply systems to ensure that front-line troops never ran out of munitions or food. Front-line troops also kept in close touch with headquarters and other units by telephone and wireless.

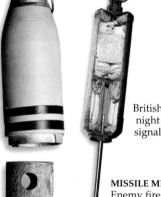

FIELD TELEPHONE
Telephones were the main communication method between the front line and headquarters. They relayed voice and Morse code messages.

GETTING IN TOUCH
Teams of engineers – such as this German group – were trained to set up, maintain, and operate telephones in the field. This allowed closer and more regular contact between the front line and HQ than in previous wars.

British night signal

MISSILE MESSAGES
Enemy fire often cut telephone lines, so both sides used shells to carry written messages. Flares on the shells lit up to signal their arrival. Signal grenades and rockets were also widely used to convey pre-arranged messages to front-line troops.

Message rolled up in base

German message shell

French army pigeon handler's badge

Canvas top secured with ropes

LOAD NOT TO EXCEED 3 TONS

WD

PIGEON POST
Carrier pigeons were often used to carry messages to and from the front line where telephone lines did not exist. In fact, the noise and confusion of the front meant that the birds easily became bewildered and flew off in the wrong direction. Germany used "war dogs" specially trained to carry messages in containers on their collars.

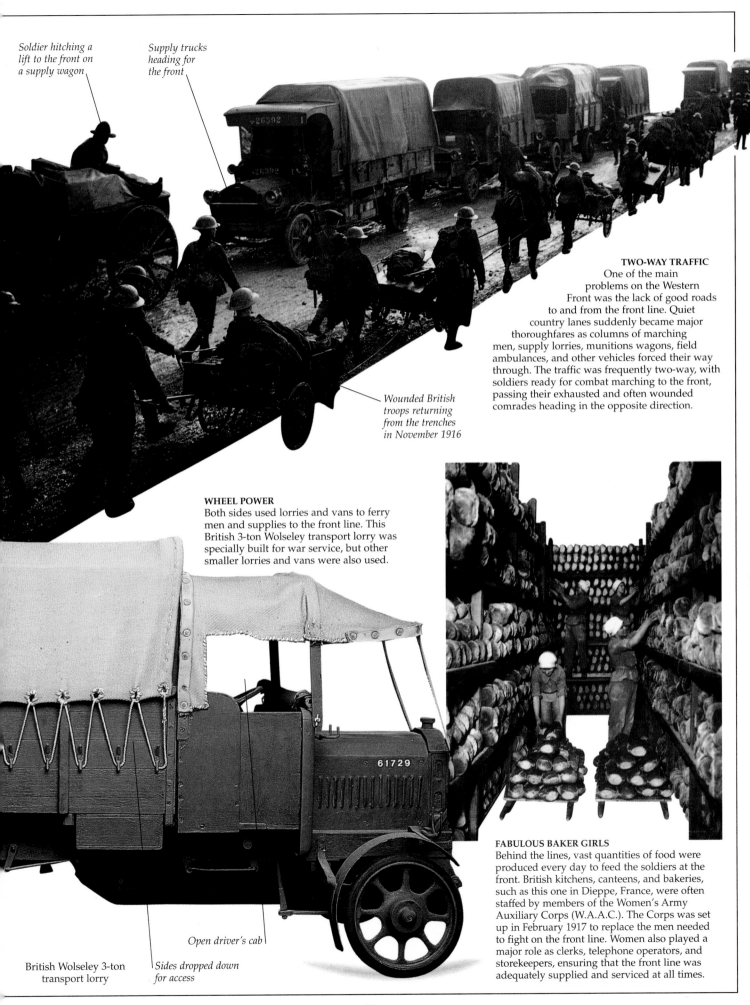

Soldier hitching a lift to the front on a supply wagon

Supply trucks heading for the front

TWO-WAY TRAFFIC
One of the main problems on the Western Front was the lack of good roads to and from the front line. Quiet country lanes suddenly became major thoroughfares as columns of marching men, supply lorries, munitions wagons, field ambulances, and other vehicles forced their way through. The traffic was frequently two-way, with soldiers ready for combat marching to the front, passing their exhausted and often wounded comrades heading in the opposite direction.

Wounded British troops returning from the trenches in November 1916

WHEEL POWER
Both sides used lorries and vans to ferry men and supplies to the front line. This British 3-ton Wolseley transport lorry was specially built for war service, but other smaller lorries and vans were also used.

Open driver's cab

British Wolseley 3-ton transport lorry

Sides dropped down for access

FABULOUS BAKER GIRLS
Behind the lines, vast quantities of food were produced every day to feed the soldiers at the front. British kitchens, canteens, and bakeries, such as this one in Dieppe, France, were often staffed by members of the Women's Army Auxiliary Corps (W.A.A.C.). The Corps was set up in February 1917 to replace the men needed to fight on the front line. Women also played a major role as clerks, telephone operators, and storekeepers, ensuring that the front line was adequately supplied and serviced at all times.

Observation and patrol

GATHERING INTELLIGENCE ABOUT the enemy is of great importance during war, because that information can be used to mount a successful attack or repel an enemy advance. Interrogating prisoners was a very successful method of gathering information. Additionally, along the Western Front, both sides were ingenious in devising new methods to gather intelligence. Night-time patrols probed the strengths and weaknesses of enemy lines. This was hazardous work, as it meant crossing rows of barbed-wire entanglements and perhaps disturbing an unexploded shell or attracting enemy gunfire. Observation turrets and periscopes were also used. Aircraft became increasingly popular since they could fly virtually unhindered over the enemy, observe their trenches and gun emplacements, and photograph the front line. This information could then be used to produce maps of the enemy lines.

Canvas wing over wooden frame

AERIAL RECONNAISSANCE
Both sides used aircraft to observe enemy positions on the Western Front. At first, Allied commanders were suspicious of this new method. But in September 1914, French Air Service pilots saw the advancing German armies change direction near Paris. This information enabled the Allies to stop the German advance into France at the Battle of the Marne. The BE2a, above and left, was strong, stable, and easy to fly, making it ideal for reconnaissance work. The craft's pilot, Lieutenant H.D. Harvey-Kelley was the first British pilot to land in France after the outbreak of war.

Leather case

Mother-of-pearl face to catch the light

Glass front

Twin-propeller engine

Twin-seater cockpit

Solid wheels

Royal Aircraft Factory Blériot Experimental (BE)2a used for reconnaissance and light bombing

COMPASS BEARINGS
A night patrol could easily get lost in no-man's-land because obvious features of the landscape, such as lanes, woods, fields, and even hills had all been blown away. A reflective compass was therefore essential if the patrol was to navigate safely and get back alive to its own trench before daybreak.

Artificial tree was an exact replica of the real tree it replaced

Soldier rests on internal step-ladder while looking through camouflaged spy-hole

German stereoscopic periscope

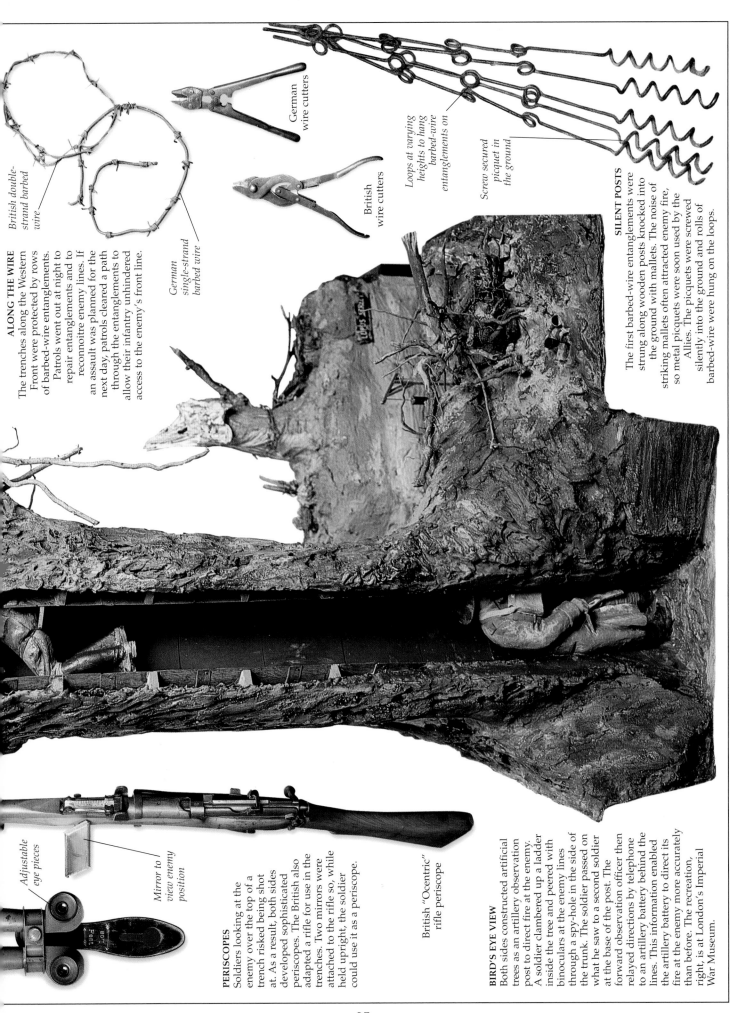

ALONG THE WIRE

The trenches along the Western Front were protected by rows of barbed-wire entanglements. Patrols went out at night to repair entanglements and to reconnoitre enemy lines. If an assault was planned for the next day, patrols cleared a path through the entanglements to allow their infantry unhindered access to the enemy's front line.

British double-strand barbed wire

German single-strand barbed wire

German wire cutters

British wire cutters

Loops at varying heights to hang barbed-wire entanglements on

Screw secured picquet in the ground

SILENT POSTS

The first barbed-wire entanglements were strung along wooden posts knocked into the ground with mallets. The noise of striking mallets often attracted enemy fire, so metal picquets were soon used by the Allies. The picquets were screwed silently into the ground and rolls of barbed-wire were hung on the loops.

PERISCOPES

Soldiers looking at the enemy over the top of a trench risked being shot at. As a result, both sides developed sophisticated periscopes. The British also adapted a rifle for use in the trenches. Two mirrors were attached to the rifle so, while held upright, the soldier could use it as a periscope.

Adjustable eye pieces

Mirror to view enemy position

British "Ocentric" rifle periscope

BIRD'S EYE VIEW

Both sides constructed artificial trees as an artillery observation post to direct fire at the enemy. A soldier clambered up a ladder inside the tree and peered with binoculars at the enemy lines through a spy-hole in the side of the trunk. The soldier passed on what he saw to a second soldier at the base of the post. The forward observation officer then relayed directions by telephone to an artillery battery behind the lines. This information enabled the artillery battery to direct its fire at the enemy more accurately than before. The recreation, right, is at London's Imperial War Museum.

Bombardment

ARTILLERY DOMINATED the battlefields of World War I. A well-aimed bombardment could destroy enemy trenches, and knock out artillery batteries and communication lines. It could also help break up an infantry attack. But as defensive positions strengthened, artillery bombardments became longer and more intense. New tactics were required to break down enemy lines. The most effective was the creeping barrage, which rained down a moving curtain of heavy and insistent fire just ahead of attacking infantry.

SIGHT SAVER
In 1916–17 a chain-mail visor was added to the basic British helmet to protect the eyes. Visors were soon removed as they were difficult to see through.

BEWARE!
Soldiers at the front needed constant reminders to keep their heads down as they were so used to shells flying past. Warning signs were common.

Helmet

Visor for extra protection

GERMAN ARMOUR
In January 1916 the German army replaced its distinctive spiked *Pickelhaube* with a rounded steel helmet. Body armour was first issued in 1916 to machine gunners.

Breastplate

Articulated plates to cover lower body

HIDING THE GUN
Two main types of artillery were used during the war – light field artillery, pulled by horses, and heavier guns, such as howitzers, moved by tractor and set up on reinforced beds. Once in place, artillery pieces were camouflaged to conceal them from the enemy.

British 8-in (20-cm) Mark V howitzer

SHELL POWER
The huge number of shells needed to maintain a constant artillery barrage against the enemy can be seen in this photograph of a British shell dump behind the Western Front.

LOADING A HOWITZER
Large pieces of artillery required a team of experienced gunners to load and fire them. This British 15-in (38-cm) howitzer was used on the Menin Road near Ypres in October 1917. The huge shell on the left of the picture is too large and heavy to lift, so it is being winched into position.

EXPLOSION!
The devasting impact of artillery fire can be seen in this dramatic picture of a British tank hit by a shell and bursting into flames. To its right, another tank breaks through the barbed wire. It was unusual for moving targets such as tanks, to be hit, and most artillery fire was used to soften up the enemy lines before an attack.

British 13-pounder (5.9-kg) high-explosive shell

French 75-mm (2.9-in) shrapnel shell

Fired from a howitzer

British 4.5-in (11.4-cm) high-explosive shell

German 15-cm (5.9-in) shrapnel shell

CLASSIFYING SHELLS
Shells were classified by weight or diameter. High-explosive shells exploded on impact. Anti-personnel shrapnel shells exploded in flight and were designed to kill or maim.

Over the top

ONCE THE ARTILLERY bombardment had pounded the enemy's defences, the infantry climbed out of their trenches and advanced towards enemy lines. The advance was very dangerous. Artillery bombardments rarely knocked out every enemy defence. Often, many gun emplacements and barbed-wire fences were still intact. Gaps in the defensive line were filled by highly mobile machine-gunners. Against them, a soldier armed with only a rifle and bayonet and laden with heavy equipment was an easy target. On the first day of the Battle of the Somme in July 1916, German machine-gun fire accounted for two British soldiers killed or injured along each metre (three feet) of the 28-km (16-mile) front.

LEAVING THE TRENCH
The most frightening moment for a soldier was scrambling up a ladder out of his trench and into no-man's-land. Few men knew the horrors that awaited them.

Steel water jacket to cool gun barrel

German MG '08 Maxim machine gun

Disc is part of the flash hider assembly, making the gun harder to spot

Trench mounting

British .303 inch Maxim Mark 3 medium machine gun

Water-cooled barrel

Tripod mounting

QUICK FIRING
Machine guns fired up to 600 bullets a minute. Ammunition was fitted into a fabric or metal-link belt, or in a metal tray fed into the gun automatically. The gun barrel was surrounded with a cold-water jacket to cool it.

IN ACTION
This German machine-gun crew is protecting the flank (side) of an advancing infantry troop on the Western Front. The reliability and firepower of machine guns made them effective weapons. Also, their small size and manoeuvrability made them difficult for the enemy to destroy.

FUTILE ATTACK

The Battle of the Somme lasted from 1 July 1916 until 18 November, when snowstorms and rain brought the attack to a muddy halt. The Allies captured about 125 sq km (48 sq miles) of land, but failed to break through the German lines, reducing much of the area to a desolate wasteland. The Germans had been on the Somme since 1914, so knew the terrain well. The British belonged to Kitchener's new army. Young and inexperienced, this was the first battle many of them had fought in.

"The sunken road ... (was) ... filled with pieces of uniform, weapons, and dead bodies."

LIEUTENANT ERNST JUNGER, GERMAN SOLDIER, THE SOMME, 1916

First day on the Somme

The Allies planned to break through the German lines north of the River Somme, France, in 1916. On 24 June, the British began a six-day artillery bombardment on German lines, but the Germans retreated into deep bunkers and were largely unharmed. As the British infantry advanced at 7.30 am on 1 July, German machine gunners emerged from their bunkers and opened fire. Believing the artillery bombardment had destroyed German lines, the infantry marched in long, slow waves towards the enemy who literally mowed them down.

TENDING THE WOUNDED

The cramped conditions in a trench can be seen in this picture of an army medical officer tending a wounded soldier at Thiepval near the Somme in September 1916. Movement along a trench was often difficult and slow.

Below: Soldiers of the 103rd (Tyneside Irish) Brigade attack La Boisselle on the first day of the Somme

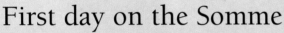

Casualty

No-one knows how many soldiers were wounded in the war, but a possible figure is 21 million. Caring for casualties was a major military operation. They were first treated at regimental aid posts in the trenches. Then, they were taken to casualty clearing stations behind the front line. Here, they received proper medical attention and basic surgery, if required, before being transported to base hospitals still further from the front. Soldiers with severe injuries went home to recover in convalescent hospitals. Over 78% of British soldiers on the Western Front returned to active service. Sickness was a major cause of casualty – in Mesopotamia over 50% of deaths were due to disease.

LUCKY MAN
Despite a splinter from a shell piercing his helmet, this soldier escaped with only a minor head wound. Many soldiers were not so fortunate, receiving severe injuries that stayed with them for life – if they survived at all.

Inventory listing contents and where to find them in the pouch

Bottles of liquid antiseptics and pain-killers

THE GERMAN KIT
German *Sanitätsmannschaften* (medical orderlies) carried two first-aid pouches on their belts. The pouch on the right (above) contained basic antiseptics, pain-killers, and other treatments, while the pouch on the left contained dressings and triangular bandages.

TRENCH AID
Injured soldiers had their wounds dressed by medical orderlies in the trench where they fell. They were then transferred to the regimental aid post, where their injuries could be assessed.

Strip of lace curtain

RECYCLED BANDAGES
Following the naval blockade by Britain, Germany ran out of cotton and linen. Wood fibre, paper, and lace curtains were used to make bandages instead.

German bandages

Forceps and clamps held securely in a metal tray

Lower tray contains saws and knives for amputation

TOOLS OF THE TRADE
Army doctors carried a standard set of surgical instruments, as in this set issued by the Indian army. Their skills were in great demand, as they faced a wide variety of injuries from bullets and shell fragments that required immediate attention.

THE FIELD HOSPITAL
Farmhouses, ruined factories, and even bombed-out churches, such as this one in Meuse, France, were used as casualty clearing stations to treat the wounded. Care was basic, and many were left to help themselves.

Shellshock

Shellshock is the collective name that was used to describe concussion, emotional shock, nervous exhaustion, and other similar ailments. Shellshock was not identified before World War I, but trench warfare was so horrific that large numbers of soldiers developed symptoms. Most of them eventually recovered, but some suffered nightmares and other effects for the rest of their lives. The condition caused great controversy, and in 1922 the British War Office Committee announced that shellshock did not exist and was a collection of already known illnesses.

A medical orderly helps a wounded soldier away from the trenches

Bunks for the injured to lie on

AMBULANCE
The British Royal Army Medical Corps, like its German counterpart, had a fleet of field ambulances to carry the wounded to hospital. Many of these ambulances were staffed by volunteers, often women, and those from non-combatant countries such as the USA.

Red Cross symbol to signify non-combatant status of the ambulance

Women at war

W HEN THE MEN went off to fight, the women were called upon to take their place. Many women were already in work, but their role was restricted to domestic labour, nursing, teaching, agricultural work on the family smallholding, and a few other jobs considered suitable for women. Now they went to work in factories, drove trucks and ambulances, and did almost everything that only men had done before. Many working women left their low-paid, low-status jobs for higher-paid work in munitions and other industries, achieving a new status in the eyes of society. Such gains, however, were short-lived, as most women returned to the home when the war ended.

ARMY LAUNDRY
Traditional pre-war women's work, such as working in a laundry or bakery, continued during the war on a much larger scale. The French women employed at this British Army laundry at Prevent, France in 1918 were washing and cleaning the dirty clothes of many thousands of soldiers every day.

FRONT-LINE ADVENTURE
For some women, the war was a big adventure. English nurse Elsie Knocker (above) went to Belgium in 1914 where she was joined by Scottish Mairi Chisholm. The women set up a dressing station at Pervyse, Belgium, and dressed the wounded until both were gassed in 1918. They were almost the only women on the front line. The two became known as the Women of Pervyse and were awarded the Order of Leopold by Belgian King Albert, and the British Military Medal. Elsie later married a Belgian officer, Baron de T'Sercles.

QUEEN MARY'S AUXILIARY
Few women actually fought in the war, but many were enlisted into auxiliary armies so that men could be released to fight on the front line. They drove trucks, mended engines, and did much of the necessary administration and supply work. In Britain, many women joined The Women's (later Queen Mary's) Army Auxiliary Corps, whose recruiting poster featured a khaki-clad woman (left) with the words "The girl behind the man behind the gun". The women remained civilians, despite their military work.

WOMEN'S LAND ARMY

The war required a huge increase in food production at home as both sides tried to restrict the enemy's imports of food from abroad. In Britain, 113,000 women joined the Women's Land Army, set up in February 1917 to provide a well-paid female workforce to run the farms. Many members of the Land Army, such as this group of healthy looking women, came from the middle and upper classes. They made a valuable contribution, but their numbers were insignificant compared with the millions of working-class women already employed on the land in the rest of Europe.

SUPPORT YOUR COUNTRY

Images of "ideal" women were used to gain support for a country's war effort. This Russian poster urges people to buy war bonds (fund-raising loans to the government) by linking Russian women to the love of the motherland.

WORKING IN POVERTY

The war brought increased status and wealth to many women but this was not the case everywhere. These Italian women worked in terrible conditions in a munitions factory. Many were very young and could not even afford shoes. This was common in factories across Italy, Germany, and Russia. The women worked long, hard hours but earned barely enough to feed their families. Strikes led by women were very common as a result.

RUSSIA'S AMAZONS

A number of Russian women joined the "Legion of Death" to fight for their country. The first battalion from Petrograd (St Petersburg) distinguished itself by taking more than 100 German prisoners during a Russian retreat, although many of the women died in the battle.

Letters to men at the front describing events at home

Family photographs

Lace handkerchief

MEMENTOS FROM HOME

Women kept in contact with their absent husbands, brothers, and sons by writing letters to them at the front. They also enclosed keepsakes, such as photographs or pressed flowers, to reassure the men that all was well in their absence and to remind them of home. Such letters and mementos did much to keep up the morale of homesick and often very frightened men.

War in the air

DOGFIGHTS
Pilots engaged in dogfights with enemy aircraft above the Western Front. Guns were mounted on top of the craft, so pilots had to fly straight at the enemy to shoot.

WHEN WAR BROKE OUT in August 1914, the history of powered flight was barely 10 years old. Aircraft had fought briefly in the Italian–Turkish war of 1911, but early aircraft development had been almost entirely for civilian use. Some military leaders could not even see how aircraft could be used in war but they soon changed their minds. The first warplanes flew as reconnaissance craft, looking down on enemy lines or helping to direct artillery fire with great precision. Enemy pilots tried to shoot them down, leading to dogfights in the sky between highly skilled and immensely brave "aces". Specialized fighter planes, such as the Sopwith Camel and the German Fokker line, were soon produced by both sides, as were sturdier craft capable of carrying bombs to drop on enemy targets. By the end of the war, the role of military aircraft had changed from being a minor help to the ground forces into a major force in their own right.

Leather face mask

Leather balaclava

Anti-splinter glass goggles

Turned-up collar to keep neck warm

Pouch to keep maps in

Coat of soft, supple leather

SOPWITH CAMEL
The Sopwith F1 Camel first flew in battle in June 1917 and became the most successful Allied fighter in shooting down German aircraft. Pilots enjoyed flying the Camel because of its exceptional agility and ability to make sharp turns at high speed.

Wooden box-structure wings covered with canvas

8.2-m (26-ft 11-in) wingspan

Sheepskin-lined leather gloves to protect against frostbite

Propeller to guide the bomb

BOMBS AWAY
The first bombs were literally dropped over the side of the aircraft by the pilot. Specialized bomber aircraft soon appeared, equipped with bombsights, bomb racks beneath the fuselage, and release systems operated by the pilot or another crew member.

DRESSED FOR THE AIR
Pilots flew in open cockpits, so they wore soft leather coats and balaclavas, sheepskin-lined fur boots, and sheepskin-lined leather gloves to keep out the cold. Later in the war, one-piece suits of waxed cotton lined with silk and fur became common.

Sheepskin boots

Thick sole to give a good grip

British 9.1-kg (20-lb) Marten Hale bomb, containing 2 kg (4.5 lb) of explosives

Fins to stop the bomb from spinning on its descent

Perforated casing to help bomb catch fire on impact

British Carcass incendiary bomb

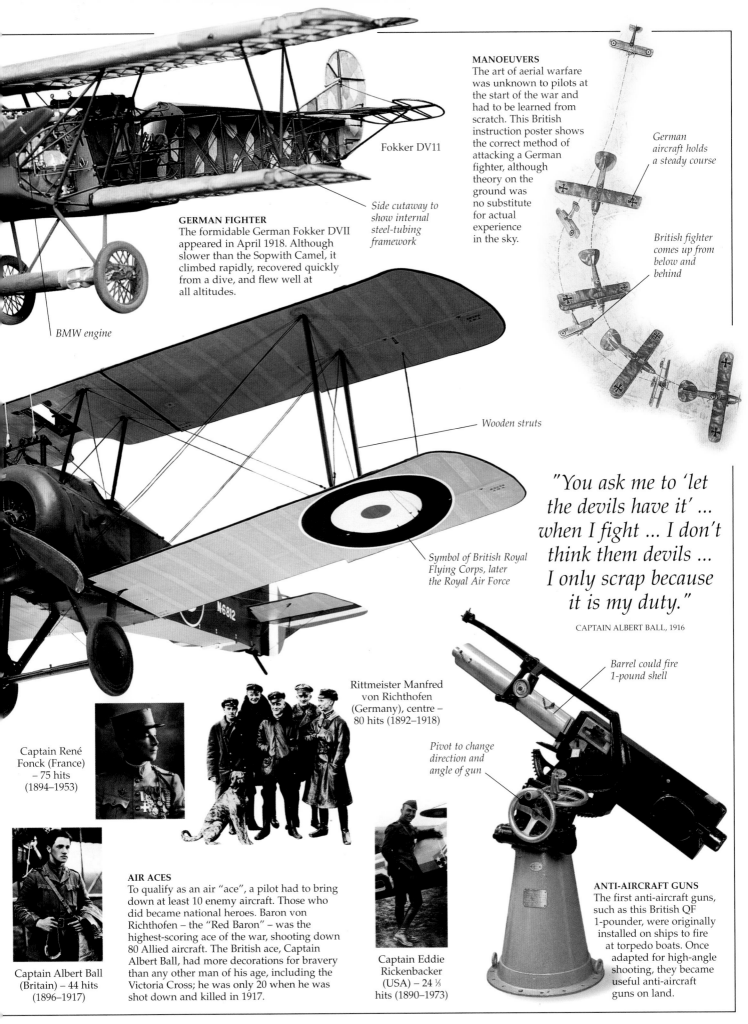

Fokker DV11

GERMAN FIGHTER
The formidable German Fokker DVII
appeared in April 1918. Although
slower than the Sopwith Camel, it
climbed rapidly, recovered quickly
from a dive, and flew well at
all altitudes.

*Side cutaway to
show internal
steel-tubing
framework*

BMW engine

MANOEUVERS
The art of aerial warfare
was unknown to pilots at
the start of the war and
had to be learned from
scratch. This British
instruction poster shows
the correct method of
attacking a German
fighter, although
theory on the
ground was
no substitute
for actual
experience
in the sky.

*German
aircraft holds
a steady course*

*British fighter
comes up from
below and
behind*

Wooden struts

*Symbol of British Royal
Flying Corps, later
the Royal Air Force*

*"You ask me to 'let
the devils have it' ...
when I fight ... I don't
think them devils ...
I only scrap because
it is my duty."*

CAPTAIN ALBERT BALL, 1916

*Barrel could fire
1-pound shell*

Rittmeister Manfred
von Richthofen
(Germany), centre –
80 hits (1892–1918)

*Pivot to change
direction and
angle of gun*

Captain René
Fonck (France)
– 75 hits
(1894–1953)

AIR ACES
To qualify as an air "ace", a pilot had to bring
down at least 10 enemy aircraft. Those who
did became national heroes. Baron von
Richthofen – the "Red Baron" – was the
highest-scoring ace of the war, shooting down
80 Allied aircraft. The British ace, Captain
Albert Ball, had more decorations for bravery
than any other man of his age, including the
Victoria Cross; he was only 20 when he was
shot down and killed in 1917.

Captain Albert Ball
(Britain) – 44 hits
(1896–1917)

Captain Eddie
Rickenbacker
(USA) – 24 ⅓
hits (1890–1973)

ANTI-AIRCRAFT GUNS
The first anti-aircraft guns,
such as this British QF
1-pounder, were originally
installed on ships to fire
at torpedo boats. Once
adapted for high-angle
shooting, they became
useful anti-aircraft
guns on land.

Zeppelin

IN THE SPRING OF 1915, the first German airships appeared in Britain's night sky. The sight of these huge, slow-moving machines caused enormous panic – at any moment a hail of bombs could fall from the airship. Yet in reality, airships played little part in the war. The first airship was designed by the German Count Ferdinand von Zeppelin in 1900. Airships are often called zeppelins, but technically only those designed by him should bear the name. Early in the war, airships could fly higher than planes, so it was almost impossible to shoot them down. This made them useful for bombing raids. But soon, higher flying aircraft and the use of incendiary (fire-making) bullets brought these aerial bombers down to earth. By 1917, most German and British airships were restricted to reconnaissance work at sea.

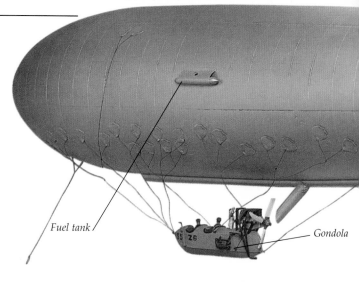

Fuel tank

Gondola

BOMBS AWAY!
Crews in the first airships had to drops their bombs, such as this incendiary bomb, over the side of the gondola by hand. Later models had automatic release mechanisms.

German incendiary bomb dropped by Zeppelin LZ38 on London, 31 May 1915

INSIDE THE GONDOLA
The crew operated the airship from the gondola – a spacious cabin below the main airship. The gondola had open sides, so the crew had little protection from the weather.

GETTING BIGGER
This L3 German airship took part in the first airship raid on Britain on the night of 19–20 January 1915, causing 20 civilian casualties. Eyewitnesses were scared by its size, but by 1918 Germany was producing ships almost three times as big.

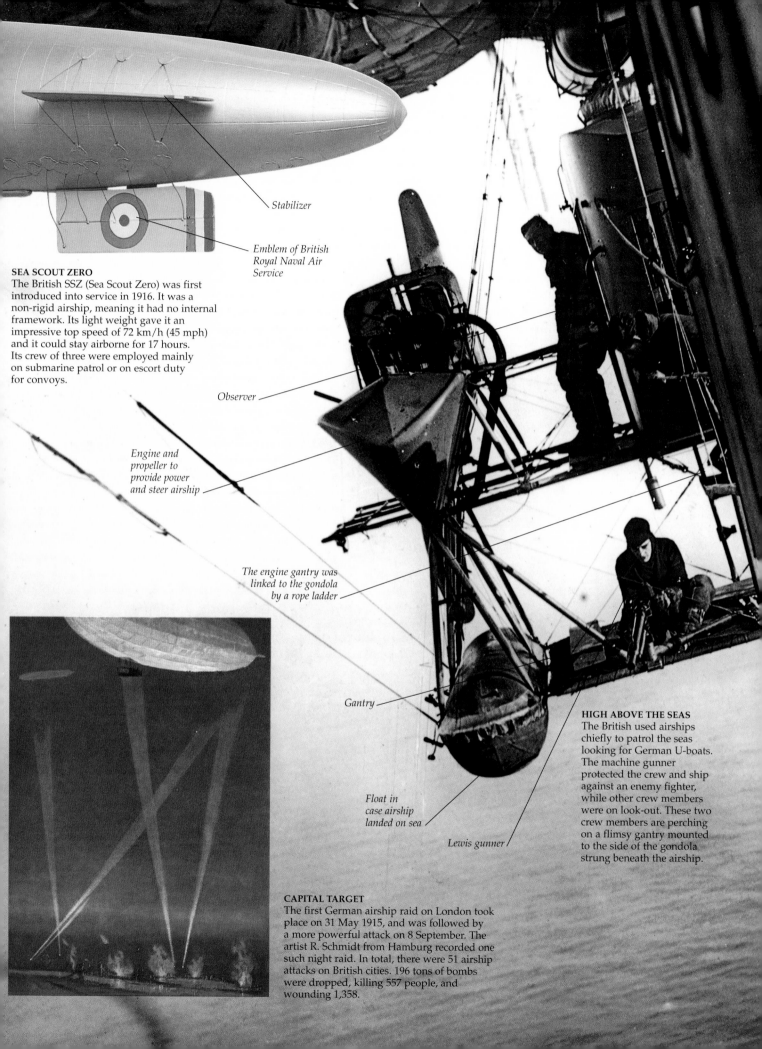

Stabilizer

Emblem of British Royal Naval Air Service

SEA SCOUT ZERO

The British SSZ (Sea Scout Zero) was first introduced into service in 1916. It was a non-rigid airship, meaning it had no internal framework. Its light weight gave it an impressive top speed of 72 km/h (45 mph) and it could stay airborne for 17 hours. Its crew of three were employed mainly on submarine patrol or on escort duty for convoys.

Observer

Engine and propeller to provide power and steer airship

The engine gantry was linked to the gondola by a rope ladder

Gantry

Float in case airship landed on sea

Lewis gunner

HIGH ABOVE THE SEAS

The British used airships chiefly to patrol the seas looking for German U-boats. The machine gunner protected the crew and ship against an enemy fighter, while other crew members were on look-out. These two crew members are perching on a flimsy gantry mounted to the side of the gondola strung beneath the airship.

CAPITAL TARGET

The first German airship raid on London took place on 31 May 1915, and was followed by a more powerful attack on 8 September. The artist R. Schmidt from Hamburg recorded one such night raid. In total, there were 51 airship attacks on British cities. 196 tons of bombs were dropped, killing 557 people, and wounding 1,358.

War at sea

Sɪɴᴄᴇ ᴛʜᴇ ʟᴀᴜɴᴄʜ ᴏғ Britain's Dreadnought
battleship in 1906, Britain, Germany, and other
countries had engaged in a massive naval
building programme. Yet the war itself was
fought largely on land and both sides avoided
naval conflict. The British needed their fleet to
keep the seas open for merchant ships bringing
food and other supplies to Britain, as well as to
prevent supplies reaching Germany. Germany
needed its fleet to protect itself against possible
invasion. The only major sea battle – off
Danish Jutland in the North Sea in 1916 – was
inconclusive. The main fight took place under
the sea, as German U-boats waged a damaging
war against Allied merchant and
troop ships in an effort to force
Britain out of the war.

CONSTANT THREAT
This German propaganda poster, *The U-boats
are out!*, shows the threat posed to Allied
shipping by the German U-boat fleet.

LIFE INSIDE A U-BOAT
Conditions inside a U-boat were
cramped and uncomfortable. Fumes
and heat from the engine and poor
ventilation made the air very stuffy.
The crew had to navigate their
craft through minefields, and avoid
detection from reconnaissance aircraft,
in order to attack enemy ships.

*Floats for
landing on
water*

LAND AND SEA
Seaplanes are able to take off and land
on both water and ground. They
were used for reconnaissance and
bombing work. This version of the
Short 184 was the first seaplane
to sink an enemy ship with
a torpedo.

*Observation
balloon*

Gun

SUCCESS AND FAILURE
German U-boats operated both under
the sea and on the surface. Here, the
crew is opening fire with a deck
cannon to stop an enemy steamer.
German U-boats sank 5,554 Allied
and neutral merchant ships as well
as many warships. Their own losses,
however, were also considerable. Out
of a total fleet of 372 German U-boats,
178 were destroyed by Allied bombs
or torpedoes.

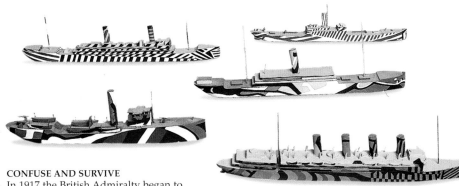

CONFUSE AND SURVIVE

In 1917 the British Admiralty began to camouflage merchant ships with strange and garish designs. These grey, black, and blue geometric patterns distorted the silhouette of the ship and made it difficult for German U-boats to determine its course and thus aim torpedoes at it with any accuracy. More than 2,700 merchant ships and 400 convoy escorts were camouflaged in this way before the war ended.

DAZZLED

During the war, many artists contributed to their country's war effort, some in surprising ways. The modern British painter Edward Wadsworth supervised the application of "dazzle" camouflage to ships' hulls. He later painted a picture (above), *Dazzle ships in dry dock at Liverpool*, showing the finished result.

Medals awarded to Jack Cornwall

Victoria Cross (VC)

British War Medal

Victory Medal

BOY (1ST CLASS)

John Travers Cornwall was only 16 when he first saw action at the Battle of Jutland on 31 May 1916. He was a ship's boy (1st class) aboard HMS *Chester* and was mortally wounded early in the battle. While other crew members lay dead or injured, Cornwall stayed at his post until the end of the action. He died of his wounds on 2 June and was posthumously awarded the Victoria Cross.

THE BRITISH GRAND FLEET

The British Royal Navy was the biggest and most powerful in the world. It operated a policy known as the "two-power standard" – the combined might of the British fleet should be the equal of the two next strongest nations combined. Despite this superiority, the navy played a fairly minor role in the war compared with the army, keeping the seas free of German ships and escorting convoys of merchant ships to Britain.

Flight deck

HMS FURIOUS

Aircraft carriers first saw service during World War I. On 7 July 1918, seven Sopwith Camels took off from the deck of HMS *Furious* to attack the zeppelin base at Tondern in northern Germany, destroying both sheds and the two Zeppelins inside.

TASTY GREETINGS
British army biscuits were often easier to write on than to eat, as this hard-baked Christmas card from Gallipoli illustrates.

Gallipoli

IN EARLY 1915 the Allies decided to force through the strategic, but heavily fortified, Dardanelles straits and capture the Ottoman Turkish capital of Constantinople. Naval attacks on 19 February and 18 March both failed. On 25 April, British, Australian, and New Zealand troops landed on the Gallipoli peninsula, while French troops staged a diversion to their south. In August, there was a second landing at Suvla Bay, also on the peninsula. Although the landings were a success, the casualty rate was high and the Allies were unable to move far from the beaches due to fierce Turkish resistance. As the months wore on, the death rate mounted. The Allies eventually withdrew in January 1916, leaving the Ottoman Empire still in control of the Dardanelles and still in the war.

GALLIPOLI PENINSULA
The Gallipoli peninsula lies to the north of the Dardanelles, a narrow waterway connecting the Aegean Sea to the Black Sea via the Sea of Marmara. Control of this waterway would have given Britain and France a direct sea route from the Mediterranean to the Black Sea and their ally, Russia. But both sides of the waterway were controlled by Germany's ally, the Ottoman Empire.

Privately purchased medical kit used by a British officer on the front line

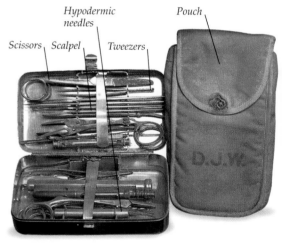

THE CASUALTY RATE
Despite the efforts of the medical staff, some of whom even carried portable surgical kits, the treatment and evacuation of casualties from Gallipoli was complicated by the enormous numbers of soldiers who were sick, as well as those who were wounded.

Jetty for boats carrying sick and wounded soldiers

THE SICK BEACH
Both sides had their food contaminated by flies carrying disease from the many corpses. Dysentery was endemic – in September 1915, 78% of the Anzac troops in the No. 1 Australian Stationary Hospital at Anzac Cove (above) were being treated for the disease.

GERMAN HELP
The Allies expected the Gallipoli peninsula to be lightly defended, but with the help of Germany, the Turks had built strong defensive positions. They dug trenches, erected barbed-wire fences, and built well-guarded artillery positions. Germany also equipped the Turks with modern pistols, rifles, and machine guns.

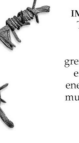

IMPROVISED GRENADES
The fighting at Gallipoli was often at very close range. Hand-thrown grenades were particularly effective in knocking out enemy positions. During a munitions shortage, Allied troops improvised by making grenades out of jam tins.

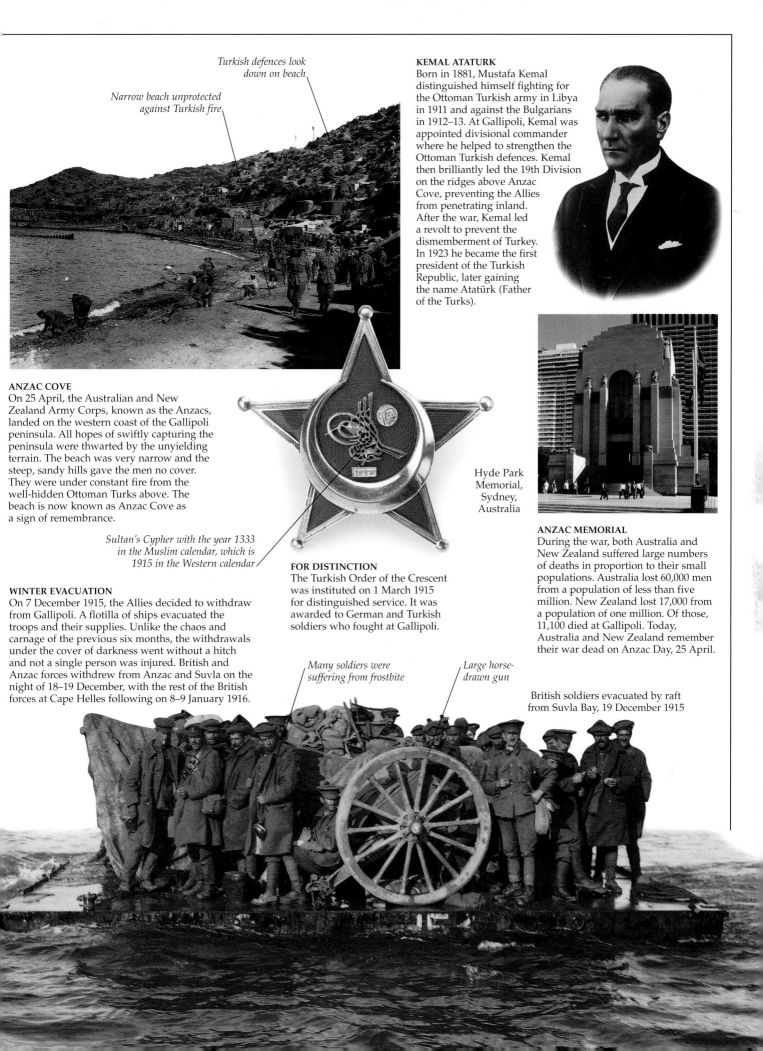

Turkish defences look down on beach

Narrow beach unprotected against Turkish fire

KEMAL ATATURK

Born in 1881, Mustafa Kemal distinguished himself fighting for the Ottoman Turkish army in Libya in 1911 and against the Bulgarians in 1912–13. At Gallipoli, Kemal was appointed divisional commander where he helped to strengthen the Ottoman Turkish defences. Kemal then brilliantly led the 19th Division on the ridges above Anzac Cove, preventing the Allies from penetrating inland. After the war, Kemal led a revolt to prevent the dismemberment of Turkey. In 1923 he became the first president of the Turkish Republic, later gaining the name Atatürk (Father of the Turks).

ANZAC COVE

On 25 April, the Australian and New Zealand Army Corps, known as the Anzacs, landed on the western coast of the Gallipoli peninsula. All hopes of swiftly capturing the peninsula were thwarted by the unyielding terrain. The beach was very narrow and the steep, sandy hills gave the men no cover. They were under constant fire from the well-hidden Ottoman Turks above. The beach is now known as Anzac Cove as a sign of remembrance.

Sultan's Cypher with the year 1333 in the Muslim calendar, which is 1915 in the Western calendar

Hyde Park Memorial, Sydney, Australia

FOR DISTINCTION

The Turkish Order of the Crescent was instituted on 1 March 1915 for distinguished service. It was awarded to German and Turkish soldiers who fought at Gallipoli.

ANZAC MEMORIAL

During the war, both Australia and New Zealand suffered large numbers of deaths in proportion to their small populations. Australia lost 60,000 men from a population of less than five million. New Zealand lost 17,000 from a population of one million. Of those, 11,100 died at Gallipoli. Today, Australia and New Zealand remember their war dead on Anzac Day, 25 April.

WINTER EVACUATION

On 7 December 1915, the Allies decided to withdraw from Gallipoli. A flotilla of ships evacuated the troops and their supplies. Unlike the chaos and carnage of the previous six months, the withdrawals under the cover of darkness went without a hitch and not a single person was injured. British and Anzac forces withdrew from Anzac and Suvla on the night of 18–19 December, with the rest of the British forces at Cape Helles following on 8–9 January 1916.

Many soldiers were suffering from frostbite

Large horse-drawn gun

British soldiers evacuated by raft from Suvla Bay, 19 December 1915

Verdun

On 21 FEBRUARY 1916, Germany launched a massive attack against Verdun, a fortified French city. Verdun lay close to the German border and controlled access into eastern France. After a huge, eight-hour artillery bombardment, the German infantry advanced. The French were caught by surprise and lost control of some of their main forts, but during the summer their resistance stiffened. By December, the Germans had been pushed back almost to where they started. The cost to both sides was enormous – over 400,000 French casualties and 336,831 German casualties. The German General Falkenhayn later claimed he had tried to bleed France to death. He did not succeed and, including losses at the Battle of the Somme, German casualties that year were 774,153.

BURNING WRECKAGE
On 25 February, the ancient city of Verdun was evacuated. Many buildings were hit by the artillery bombardment, and even more destroyed by the fires that raged often for days. Firefighters did their best to control the blazes, but large numbers of houses had wooden frames and burned easily.

GENERAL PETAIN
General Henri-Philippe Pétain took command of the French forces of Verdun on 25 February, the same day as the loss of Fort Douaumont. He organized an effective defence of the town and made sure the army was properly supplied. His rallying cry, "Ils ne passeront pas!" (They shall not pass!), did much to raise French morale.

Exposed concrete fort wall

Machine-gun post

Double-breasted greatcoat

Horizon-blue uniform

Haversack

Lebel rifle

Steel helmet

Thick boots with puttees wrapped around the legs

FORT DOUAUMONT
Verdun was protected by three rings of fortifications. Fort Douaumont, in the outer ring, was the strongest of these forts. It was built of steel and concrete and surrounded by ramparts, ditches, and rolls of barbed wire. But although the fort itself was strong, it was defended by just 56 elderly reservists. The fort fell to the Germans on 25 February.

Background picture: Ruined Verdun cityscape, 1915

LE POILU
The French slang for an infantry soldier was *le poilu*, or "hairy one". *Les poilus* bore the brunt of the German attack, enduring the muddy, cold, and wet conditions and suffering dreadful injuries from shellfire and poison gas.

AT CLOSE QUARTERS

Fighting at Verdun was particularly fierce, as both sides repeatedly attacked and counter-attacked the same forts and strategic areas around the city. Advancing attackers were assaulted by hails of machine-gun fire from the enemy within the forts. The open ground was so exposed that it was impossible to retrieve the dead, and corpses were left to rot in the ground. The forts were also riddled with underground tunnels where both sides engaged in vicious hand-to-hand combat. Many dramatic films have been made about the war, and this photograph comes from one such film.

> *"What a bloodbath, what horrid images, what a slaughter. I just cannot find the words to express my feelings. Hell cannot be this dreadful."*
>
> ALBERT JOUBAIRE
> FRENCH SOLDIER, VERDUN, 1916

SURROUNDING VILLAGES

The village of Ornes was one of many French villages attacked and captured during the German advance on Verdun. The devastation was so great that this village, along with eight others, was not rebuilt after the war, but is still marked on maps as a sign of remembrance.

Laurel-leaf wreath

Oak-leaf wreath

Head of Marianne, symbol of France

LEGION D'HONNEUR

In recognition of the suffering experienced by Verdun's people, French president Raymond Poincaré awarded the city the *Légion d'Honneur*. The honour is usually presented to men and women, military and civilian, for bravery.

THE MUDDY INFERNO

The countryside around Verdun is wooded and hilly, with many streams running down to the River Meuse. Heavy rainfall and constant artillery bombardment turned this landscape into a desolate mudbath, where the bodies of the dead lay half-buried in shell craters and men were forced to eat and sleep within inches of their fallen comrades. This photograph shows the "Ravine de la mort", the Ravine of the Dead.

British "Hypo" helmet

Gas attack

ON THE AFTERNOON of 22 April 1915, French-Algerian troops near the Belgian town of Ypres noticed a greenish-yellow cloud moving towards them from the German front. The cloud was chlorine gas. This was the first time poison gas had been used effectively in war. As it reached the Allied line, many soldiers panicked, for they had no protection against its choking effects. Over the next three years, both sides used gas – the Germans released about 68,000 tonnes, the British and French 51,000 tonnes. The first gas clouds were released from canisters and blown by the wind towards the enemy, but this caused problems if the wind changed and blew the gas in the wrong direction. More effective were gas-filled shells, which could be targeted at enemy lines. In total, 1,200,000 soldiers on both sides were gassed, of whom 91,198 died terrible deaths.

EARLY WARNING
The first anti-gas masks were crude and often ineffectual, as these instructional drawings from a British training school show. Basic goggles protected the eyes, while mouth-pads made of flannel or other absorbent materials were worn over the mouth. Chemicals soaked into the pads neutralized the gas.

British anti-gas goggles

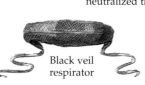

Black veil respirator

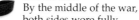

Flannel respirator

Air tube

Chemical filter to neutralize gas

ALL-IN-ONE
By the middle of the war, both sides wore fully protective helmets, which consisted of face masks, goggles, and respirators. These protected the eyes, nose, and throat from the potentially lethal effects of gas.

British smallbox respirator

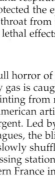

Gas alarm whistle

GASSED!
The full horror of being blinded by gas is caught in *Gassed*, a painting from real life by the American artist John Singer Sargent. Led by their sighted colleagues, the blinded soldiers are slowly shuffling towards a dressing station near Arras in northern France in August 1918.

GAS SHELLS

Lachrymatory | Phosgene & Diphosgene | Diphosgene & Sneezing Oil | Diphosgene | Mustard Oil

Gas shells contained liquid gas, which evaporated on impact. Gases caused a range of injuries depending on their type. Gases such as chlorine, diphosgene, and phosgene caused severe breathing difficulties while benzyl bromide caused the eyes to water. Dichlorethylsulphide burned and blistered the skin, caused temporary blindness and, if inhaled, flooded the lungs and led to death from pneumonia.

Glove shrunken by gas

Ordinary glove

UNDER ATTACK

The first effects of gas were felt on the face and in the eyes, but within seconds it entered the throat. Soldiers coughed and choked as the gas swirled around them. The longterm effects depended on the type of gas used – some soldiers died very quickly, others were blinded for life or suffered awful skin blisters, while some died a lingering death as their lungs collapsed and filled with liquid. The only protection was to wear combined goggles and respirator. Major Tracy Evert photographed these American soldiers in 1918. They are posing to illustrate the ill effects of forgetting their gas masks. The photograph was used when training new recruits.

HAND SHRUNK

When exposed to some kinds of gas, a glove like the one above will shrink to the size of the glove above, right. This is what happens to a person's lungs when exposed to the same gas.

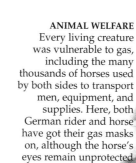

German gas mask

Eyes not protected

Canvas-covered respirator

ANIMAL WELFARE

Every living creature was vulnerable to gas, including the many thousands of horses used by both sides to transport men, equipment, and supplies. Here, both German rider and horse have got their gas masks on, although the horse's eyes remain unprotected and vulnerable.

The Eastern Front

TANNENBERG, 1914
In August 1914, Russia's First and Second armies invaded East Prussia, Germany. The Russians did not disguise their messages in code, so the Germans knew what to expect. The Second Army was soon surrounded at Tannenberg and was forced to surrender on 31 August, with the loss of 150,000 men and all of its artillery (above).

WHEN PEOPLE THINK today of World War I, they picture the fighting in the trenches along the Western Front. But on the other side of Europe, a very different war took place, between Germany and Austria-Hungary on one side and Russia on the other. This war was much more fluid, with great armies marching backwards and forwards across many hundreds of kilometres. Both the Austro-Hungarian and Russian armies were badly led and poorly equipped, and both suffered huge losses. In 1915 alone, the Russians lost two million men, of whom one million were taken prisoner. The German army, ably led by General Hindenburg, was far more effective. By the end of 1916, despite some Russian successes, the Germans were in full control of the entire Eastern Front. The Russians were greatly demoralized and this led, in part, to the Russian Revolution the following year, 1917.

MASURIAN LAKES, 1914
In September 1914, the Russian First Army had marched to the Masurian Lakes in East Prussia. It was in danger of being surrounded as the Second Army had been the previous month at Tannenberg. German troops dug trenches and other defences (above) and attacked the Russians, who soon withdrew, sustaining more than 100,000 casualties. By the end of September, the Russian threat to Germany was over.

INITIAL SUCCESS
During 1914 the Russian army conquered Austria-Hungary's eastern province of Galicia, inflicting huge defeats on the Austro-Hungarian army. But, in 1915, German reinforcements (above) pushed the Russians back into their own country.

The Italian Front

On 23 May 1915, Italy joined the war on the side of the Allies and prepared to invade its hostile neighbour, Austria-Hungary. Fighting took place on two fronts – north and east. Italy fought against the Italian-speaking Trentino region of Austria-Hungary to the north, and along the Isonzo River to the east. The Italian army was ill-prepared and under-equipped for the war, and was unable to break through the Austrian defences until its final success at the Battle of Vittorio-Veneto in October 1918.

UNWILLING TO FIGHT

By the end of 1916, many Russian soldiers were refusing to fight. They were badly treated, ill-equipped, poorly led, and starving. They saw little reason to risk their lives in a war they did not believe in. Officers had to threaten their troops to make them fight, and mutinies were common, although many thousands simply deserted and went home.

Below: Russian troops marching to defend the newly captured city of Przemysl in Austrian Galicia

THE ISONZO

The Isonzo River formed a natural boundary between the mountains of Austria-Hungary and the plains of northern Italy. Between June 1915 and August 1917, the two sides fought 11 inconclusive battles along the river before the Austrians, with German support, achieved a decisive victory at Caporetto in December 1917.

ITALIAN ALPINISTS

All but 32 km (20 miles) of the 640-km (400-mile) Italian frontier with Austria-Hungary lay in the Italian Alps. Both sides used trained alpine troops to fight in mountainous terrain. Every mountain peak became a potential observation post or gun emplacement.

War in the desert

FIGHTING DURING World War I was not restricted just to Europe. German colonies in Africa were overrun by French, British, and South African forces, while Germany's colonies in China and the Pacific were invaded by Japanese, British, Australian, and New Zealand forces. One of the major conflicts took place in the Middle East. Here, the Turkish Ottoman Empire controlled Mesopotamia (modern Iraq), Palestine, Syria, and Arabia. British and Indian troops invaded Mesopotamia in 1914 and finally captured Baghdad in 1917. Meanwhile, a large British force, under General Allenby, captured Palestine and, in the last weeks of the war, the Syrian capital of Damascus. In Arabia, Bedouin soldiers under the guidance of T.E. Lawrence rose in revolt against their Turkish rulers and waged a guerrilla campaign for an independent Arab state.

SPINE PAD
The British army was concerned that soldiers fighting in the desert might get heatstroke. They therefore issued spine pads to protect the soldiers' backs from the sun. The weight and discomfort of the pad would have done little to keep the body cool.

Arab flintlock pistol

Lawrence's rifle

Lawrence's initials

RETURN JOURNEY
British soldier T.E. Lawrence's rifle was one of the many British rifles captured by the Turks at Gallipoli in 1915. It was then given by the Turkish War Minister, Enver Pasha, to the Arab leader, Emir Feisal, who in turn presented it to Lawrence in December 1916.

LAWRENCE OF ARABIA
The British soldier T.E. Lawrence is a romantic, almost legendary figure known as Lawrence of Arabia. Lawrence first visited the Middle East in 1909, and learned to speak Arabic. In 1914 he became an army intelligence officer in Cairo, Egypt. Later, he worked as liaison officer to Emir Feisal, leader of the Arab revolt against Ottoman Turkish rule. Lawrence helped the Arabs to become an effective guerrilla force, blowing up railway lines, attacking Turkish garrisons, and tying down an army many times their own size.

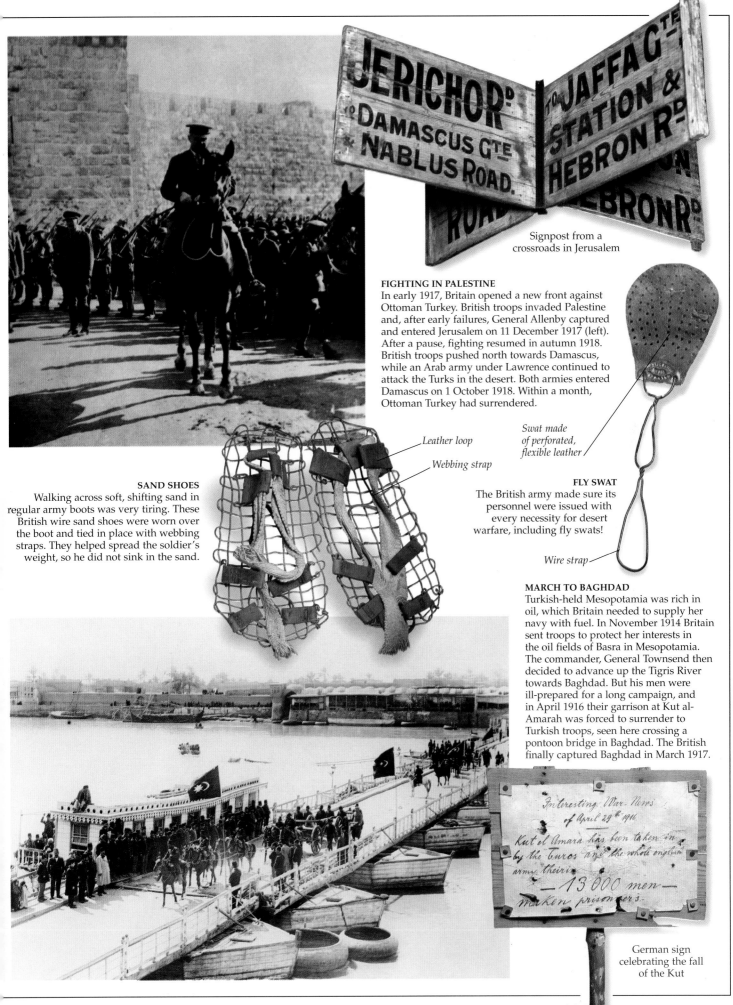

Signpost from a
crossroads in Jerusalem

FIGHTING IN PALESTINE
In early 1917, Britain opened a new front against Ottoman Turkey. British troops invaded Palestine and, after early failures, General Allenby captured and entered Jerusalem on 11 December 1917 (left). After a pause, fighting resumed in autumn 1918. British troops pushed north towards Damascus, while an Arab army under Lawrence continued to attack the Turks in the desert. Both armies entered Damascus on 1 October 1918. Within a month, Ottoman Turkey had surrendered.

Leather loop

Webbing strap

Swat made
of perforated,
flexible leather

SAND SHOES
Walking across soft, shifting sand in regular army boots was very tiring. These British wire sand shoes were worn over the boot and tied in place with webbing straps. They helped spread the soldier's weight, so he did not sink in the sand.

FLY SWAT
The British army made sure its personnel were issued with every necessity for desert warfare, including fly swats!

Wire strap

MARCH TO BAGHDAD
Turkish-held Mesopotamia was rich in oil, which Britain needed to supply her navy with fuel. In November 1914 Britain sent troops to protect her interests in the oil fields of Basra in Mesopotamia. The commander, General Townsend then decided to advance up the Tigris River towards Baghdad. But his men were ill-prepared for a long campaign, and in April 1916 their garrison at Kut al-Amarah was forced to surrender to Turkish troops, seen here crossing a pontoon bridge in Baghdad. The British finally captured Baghdad in March 1917.

Interesting War News
of April 29th 1916.

Kut el Amara has been taken in
by the Turcs and the whole english
army theiris
—13.000 men—
taken prisoners.

German sign
celebrating the fall
of the Kut

Espionage

BOTH SIDES SUSPECTED the other of employing hundreds of spies to report on enemy intentions and capabilities. In fact, most espionage work consisted not of spying on enemy territory but of eavesdropping on enemy communications. Code-breaking or cryptography was very important as both sides sent and received coded messages by radio and telegraph. Cryptographers devised highly complex codes to ensure the safe transit of their own messages while using their skills to intercept and break coded enemy messages. Such skills enabled British intelligence to decipher the Zimmermann telegram from Berlin to Washington sent in January 1917, leading to the entry of the USA into the war in April 1917.

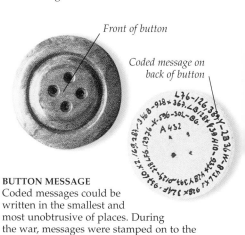

Lightweight, but strong, string attaches parachute to bird

Corselet made of linen and padded to protect bird

PIGEON POST

Over 500,000 pigeons were used during the war to carry messages between intelligence agents and their home bases. The pigeons were dropped by parachute into occupied areas. Agents collected the pigeons at drop zones and looked after them until they had information to send home. When released, the birds flew home to their lofts with messages attached to their legs.

IN MINIATURE

Pigeons could not carry much weight, so messages had to be written on small pieces of paper. This message, in German, is written on a standard "pigeon post" form used by the German army. Long messages could be photographed with a special camera that reduced them to the size of a microdot – that is 300 hundred times smaller than the original.

EDITH CAVELL

Edith Cavell was born in England and worked as a governess in Belgium in the early 1890s before training in England as a nurse. In 1907 she returned to Belgium to start a nursing school in Brussels (above). When the Germans occupied the city in August 1914 she decided to stay, accommodating up to 200 British soldiers who also found themselves behind enemy lines. The Germans arrested her and tried her for "conducting soldiers to the enemy". She was found guilty and executed by firing squad in October 1915. Cavell was not a spy, but her execution did provide a powerful propaganda weapon for the Allies.

Front of button

Coded message on back of button

SECRET INK

Invisible ink was used to conceal messages written on paper. The invisible message could be read later when the paper was treated with a chemical to make the words visible.

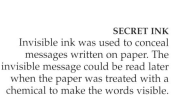

German invisible ink and sponge

Invisible ink bottle

BUTTON MESSAGE

Coded messages could be written in the smallest and most unobtrusive of places. During the war, messages were stamped on to the back of buttons sewn onto coats or jackets.

POCKET CAMERA
Small cameras hidden in a pocket or disguised as a fob watch were used to take clandestine photographs. This spy camera saw service in German East Africa (now Tanzania).

Lens cap

Camera lens

Shutter release

READING THE ENEMY
Army intelligence officers, such as this British soldier, played a vital role in examining and understanding captured enemy documents. Painstaking reading of every piece of information enabled the intelligence services to build up a reasonably complete picture about enemy preparations for an attack. They could also assess the state of civilian morale, and pass that information on to the military high command.

HIDDEN MESSAGES
Not every spy remained undetected. Two agents from the Netherlands sent to Portsmouth, England, to spy for Germany pretended to be cigar importers. They used their orders for imported Dutch cigars as codes for the ships they observed in Portsmouth Harbour. They were caught and executed in 1915.

Cigars slit open in search of hidden messages

AID TO ESCAPE
This tin, supposedly containing ox tongue, was sent to British Lieutenant Jack Shaw at the German Prisoner of War Camp, Holzminden in 1918. It contained maps, wire cutters, and compasses to help Shaw arrange a mass escape from the camp.

Rolled-up map of France

Lead weights to make the tin the correct weight

Compass

MATA HARI
Dutch-born Margaretta Zelle was a famous dancer who used the stage-name Mata Hari. She had many high-ranking lovers, which enabled her to pass on any confidential information she acquired from them to the secret services. In 1914, while dancing in Paris, she was recruited by the French intelligence service. She went to Madrid, where she tried to win over a German diplomat. He double-crossed her with false information and on her return to France she was arrested, tried, and found guilty of being a German agent. She was executed by firing squad in October 1917.

Tank warfare

THE BRITISH-INVENTED tank was a major mechanical innovation of the war. British tanks first saw action in September 1916, but these early tanks were not very reliable. It was not until November 1917, at the Battle of Cambrai, that their full potential was realized. At Cambrai, the German defences were so strong that an artillery bombardment would have destroyed the ground and made it impossible for the infantry to cross. Instead, fleets of tanks flattened barbed-wire, crossed enemy trenches, and acted as shields for the advancing infantry. Tanks played a vital role in the allied advances throughout 1918.

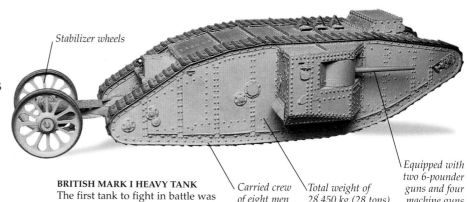

Stabilizer wheels

Carried crew of eight men

Total weight of 28,450 kg (28 tons)

Equipped with two 6-pounder guns and four machine guns

BRITISH MARK I HEAVY TANK
The first tank to fight in battle was the British Mark 1 tank. Forty-nine were ready to fight at the Battle of the Somme on 15 September 1916, but only 18 were reliable enough to take part in the battle itself.

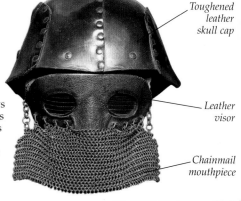

Toughened leather skull cap

Leather visor

Chainmail mouthpiece

PROTECT AND SURVIVE
Leather helmets, faceguards, and chainmail mouthpieces were issued to British tank crews to protect their heads. The visors gave protection against particles of hot metal which flew off the inside of the hull when the tank was hit by a bullet.

German A7V tank

A7V TANK
The only German tank built during the war was the huge A7V, a 33,500-kg (33-ton) machine with six machine guns and a crew of 18. Only 20 A7Vs were constructed, and their appearance in spring 1918 was too late in the war to make any real impact.

British Mark V tank

INSIDE A TANK
Life inside a tank was very unpleasant. The tank was hot, fume-ridden, and badly ventilated, making the crew sick or even faint. The heat was sometimes so great in light tanks that it exploded the ammunition.

Rear entry hatch

Driver's entry hatch

Lid for driver's entry hatch

Driver's visor

T 9171

Iron caterpillar track

The driver and gunner were squashed in the front of the tank

Six men sat around the engine manning the guns

Six-cylinder engine

BRITISH MARK V TANK
The British Mark V tank first saw action in July 1918. It was equipped with two 6-pounder guns and four machine guns, and had a crew of eight. Its advanced system of gears and brakes allowed it to be driven and controlled by only one person.

Machine-gun port

DRIVING A TANK
The first British tanks were driven by two people, each controlling one track. They had a limited range of 40 km (24 miles) and their tracks broke regularly. Later tanks were driven by a single person and were more manoeuvrable and robust. However, they were still vulnerable to enemy shellfire, and often broke down, as here during the British assault on Arras in April 1917.

CROSSING THE TRENCHES
A tank could cross a narrow trench easily, but it could topple into a wide one. To solve this problem, the British equipped their tanks with circular metal bundles that could be dropped into a trench to form a bridge. Here, a line of Mark V tanks are moving in to attack German trenches during autumn 1918.

The US enters the war

British medal suggesting the attack on SS *Lusitania* was planned

Wᴴᴇɴ ᴡᴀʀ broke out in Europe in August 1914, the USA remained neutral. The country was deeply divided about the war, as many of its citizens had recently arrived from Europe and were strongly in favour of one side or the other. When German U-boats started to sink American ships, however, public opinion began to turn against Germany. In February 1917, Germany decided to attack all foreign shipping to try to reduce supplies to Britain. It also tried to divert US attention from Europe by encouraging its neighbour, Mexico, to invade. This action outraged the US government, and as more US ships were sunk, President Wilson declared war on Germany. This was now a world war.

UNCLE SAM
The artist James Montgomery Flagg used himself as a model for Uncle Sam, a cartoon figure intended to represent every American. The portrait was based on Kitchener's similar pose for British recruiting posters (see page 14). Beneath his pointing finger were the words "I WANT YOU FOR THE US ARMY".

SS LUSITANIA
On 7 May 1915 the passenger ship SS *Lusitania* was sunk off the coast of Ireland by German torpedoes because the ship was suspected of carrying munitions. The ship was bound from New York, USA, to Liverpool, England. Three-quarters of the passengers drowned, including 128 US citizens. Their death did much to turn the US public against Germany and towards the Allies.

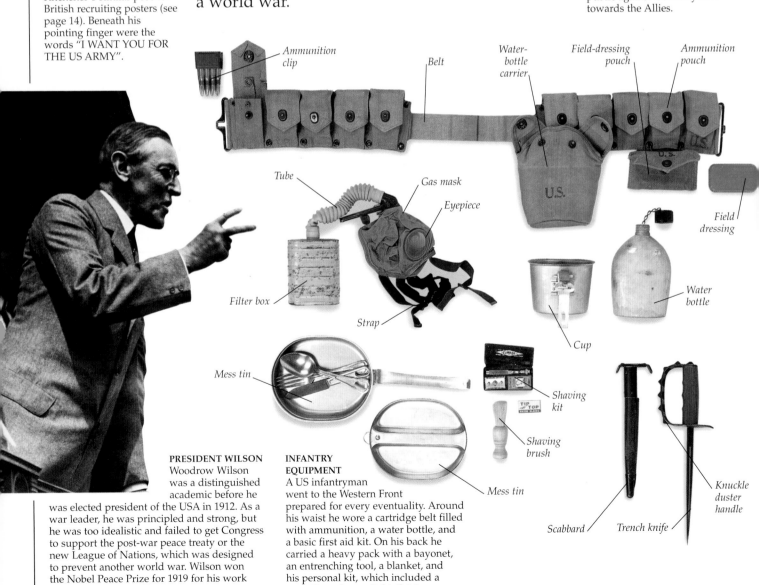

Ammunition clip

Belt

Water-bottle carrier

Field-dressing pouch

Ammunition pouch

Tube

Gas mask

Eyepiece

Field dressing

Filter box

Strap

Cup

Water bottle

Mess tin

Shaving kit

Shaving brush

Mess tin

Scabbard

Trench knife

Knuckle duster handle

PRESIDENT WILSON
Woodrow Wilson was a distinguished academic before he was elected president of the USA in 1912. As a war leader, he was principled and strong, but he was too idealistic and failed to get Congress to support the post-war peace treaty or the new League of Nations, which was designed to prevent another world war. Wilson won the Nobel Peace Prize for 1919 for his work in bringing peace to Europe.

INFANTRY EQUIPMENT
A US infantryman went to the Western Front prepared for every eventuality. Around his waist he wore a cartridge belt filled with ammunition, a water bottle, and a basic first aid kit. On his back he carried a heavy pack with a bayonet, an entrenching tool, a blanket, and his personal kit, which included a mess tin and essential toiletries.

GUN FIRE

The US First Army saw its first major action on 12–16 September 1918 at St Mihiel, south of Verdun, France, as part of a combined Allied attack against German lines. Here an artillery crew fires a 75-mm field gun as a spent shell-case flies through the air.

FOR HEROISM

Instituted by Presidential Order in 1918, the Distinguished Service Cross was awarded for extreme heroism against an armed enemy.

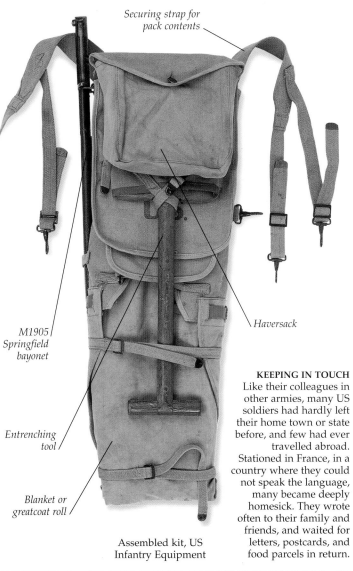

Securing strap for pack contents

Haversack

M1905 Springfield bayonet

Entrenching tool

Blanket or greatcoat roll

Assembled kit, US Infantry Equipment

KEEPING IN TOUCH

Like their colleagues in other armies, many US soldiers had hardly left their home town or state before, and few had ever travelled abroad. Stationed in France, in a country where they could not speak the language, many became deeply homesick. They wrote often to their family and friends, and waited for letters, postcards, and food parcels in return.

Under enemy lines

Air tubes

TO THE RESCUE
A gas attack or a shell burst near a mine tunnel entrance could fill the mine with fumes, suffocating the men working inside. This German breathing apparatus was kept on standby for use by rescue parties.

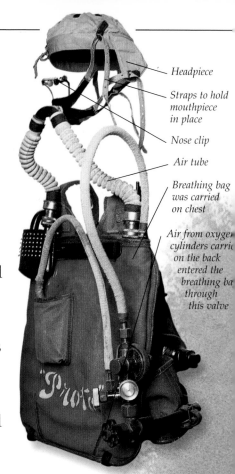

Headpiece

Straps to hold mouthpiece in place

Nose clip

Air tube

Breathing bag was carried on chest

Air from oxygen cylinders carried on the back entered the breathing bag through this valve

FOR MUCH OF the war on the Western Front, the two sides faced each other in rows of heavily fortified trenches. These massive defences were very difficult to overcome, so engineers found ways of undermining them. The British army recruited coal miners and "clay-kickers", who used to dig tunnels for London Underground. The Germans had their own miners. Both excavated tunnels and mines deep under enemy lines and packed them with explosives, ready to be detonated when an attack began. Counter-mines were also dug to cut into and destroy enemy mines before they could be finished. The opposing miners sometimes met and fought in underground battles. Vast mines were exploded by the British at the Battle of the Somme on 1 July 1916, but their most effective use was under Messines Ridge at the start of the Battle of Passchendaele.

OXYGEN RELIEF
This British breathing apparatus is similar to the German equipment on the left. Compressed oxygen contained in the breathing bags was released through the air tubes to help the miner breathe.

Background picture: One of many British mines explodes under German lines at the Battle of the Somme, 1 July 1916

SAPPERS AT WORK
British artist David Bomberg's painting shows members of the Royal Engineers, known as sappers, digging and reinforcing an underground trench. Sappers ensured that trenches and tunnels were properly constructed and did not collapse.

"It is horrible. You often wish you were dead, there is no shelter, we are lying in water ... our clothes do not dry."

GERMAN SOLDIER, PASSCHENDAELE, 1917

WATERLOGGED
The water table around Ypres was very high, so the trenches were built above ground by banking up earth and sandbags. Even so, the trenches were constantly flooded. Pumping out mines and trenches, as these Australian tunnellers are doing at Hooge, Belgium in September 1917, was an essential, never-ending task.

Passchendaele

During 1917, the British planned a massive attack against the German front line around Ypres, Belgium. They aimed to break into Belgium and capture the channel ports, stopping the German submarines from using them as a base to attack British shipping. The Battle of Messines began on 7 June 1917. After a huge artillery bombardment, 19 mines packed with 1 million tons of explosive blew up simultaneously under the German lines on Messines Ridge. The noise could be heard in London 220 km (140 miles) away. The ridge was soon captured, but the British failed to take quick advantage. Heavy rainfall in August and October turned the battlefield into a muddy marshland. The village and ridge of Passchendaele were eventually captured on 10 November 1917, only to be lost again the following March. In summer 1918, the Allies re-captured and kept the ground.

MUDDY QUAGMIRE
Heavy rainfall and constant shelling at Passchendaele created a deadly mudbath. Many injured men died as they were unable to lift themselves clear of the cloying mud. Stretcher bearers were barely able to carry the wounded to dressing stations. The British poet Siegfried Sassoon, wrote that "I died in hell – (They called it Passchendaele)".

Below: British troops moving forward over shell-torn ground during the Battle of Passchendaele.

The final year

IN EARLY 1918, the war looked to be turning in favour of Germany and her allies. Russia had withdrawn from the war, enabling Germany to concentrate her efforts on the Western Front, and US troops had yet to arrive in France in any great numbers. A vast offensive in March brought German troops to within 64 km (40 miles) of Paris. But behind the lines, Germany was far from strong. The Allied blockade of German ports meant that the country was short of vital supplies. The railway network was collapsing through lack of maintenance and food was short. Strikes and even mutinies became common. Elsewhere, Ottoman Turkey and Bulgaria collapsed in the face of Allied attacks, while the Italians scored a decisive victory against Austria-Hungary. By early November, Germany stood alone. On 7 November, a German delegation crossed the front line to discuss peace terms with the Allies. The war was almost over.

NEW LEADER
In 1917, Vladimir Lenin, the leader of the Bolshevik (Communist) Party, became the new ruler of Russia. He was opposed to the war, and ordered an immediate cease-fire when he came to power.

German and Russian troops celebrating the cease-fire on the Eastern Front, 1917

Russia pulls out

The Russian government became increasingly unpopular as the war progressed. The army was demoralized by constant defeats, and by early 1917, there was large-scale fraternization with German troops along the Eastern Front. In February 1917, a revolution overthrew the Tsar, but the new government continued the war. A second revolution in October brought the Bolshevik Party to power. A cease-fire was agreed with Germany, and in March 1918 Russia signed the Treaty of Brest-Litovsk and withdrew from the war.

THE LUDENDORFF OFFENSIVE
On 21 March 1918 General Ludendorff launched a huge attack on the Western Front. He hoped to defeat Britain and France before US reinforcements could arrive. The attack took the Allies by surprise and Germany advanced by almost 64 km (40 miles) by July, but at the heavy cost of 500,000 casualties.

French and British troops in action during the Ludendorff Offensive

8 January US President Wilson issues 14 Points for Peace
3 March Treaty of Brest-Litovsk – Russia leaves the war
21 March Vast German Ludendorff offensive on the Western Front
15 July Last German offensive launched on Western Front
18 July French counter-attack begins on the Marne
8 August British launch offensive near Amiens
12 September Americans launch offensive at St Mihiel
14 September Allies attack Bulgarians at Salonika
25 September Bulgaria seeks peace
27 September British begin to breach Hindenburg Line

BATTLE OF THE MARNE

On 18 July 1918, French and US forces, led by General Foch, counter-attacked against the German advance on the River Marne, east of Paris. They stopped the German offensive in its tracks and began to push the Germans back eastwards. By 6 August, the Germans had lost 168,000 men, many buried where they fell on the battlefields (left). The tide of battle had at last turned decisively in favour of the Allied armies.

French soldiers identifying German dead before burial

CROSSING THE LINE

On 8 August 1918 a massive British offensive began near Amiens. The German army was increasingly short of men and vital supplies, including food, so gave little resistance. The Allied troops continued to push forwards towards the heavily fortified Hindenburg Line. On 29 September, the British 46th North Midland Division captured the bridge at Riqueval, over the St Quentin Canal. They posed for a celebratory photograph, because they had broken the Line at last.

Many French children did not remember life before the German occupation of their towns and cities

Background picture: German troops advancing at the Somme, April 1918

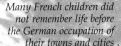

French children march alongside the Allied army

THE LAST DAYS

By 5 October, the Allied armies had breached the entire Hindenburg Line and were crossing open country. Both sides suffered great casualties as the German army was pushed steadily eastwards. The British and French recaptured towns and cities lost in 1914, including Lille (left), and by early November 1918 they recaptured Mons, where they had fired the first shots of the war in August 1914. By now, the German retreat was turning into a rout.

28 September German commander Ludendorff advises the Kaiser to seek peace as army crumbles
1 October British capture Ottoman Turkish-held Damascus

6 October German government starts to negotiate an armistice
21 October Czechoslovakia declares its independence
24 October Italian army begins

decisive battle of Vittorio-Veneto against Austria-Hungary
29 October German fleet mutinies
30 October Ottoman Turkey agrees an armistice

4 November Austria-Hungary agrees an armistice
9 November The Kaiser abdicates
11 November Armistice between Germany and the Allies; war ends

Armistice and peace

CARRIAGE TALKS
On 7 November 1918, a German delegation headed by a government minister, Matthias Erzberger, crossed the front line to meet the Allied commander-in-chief, Marshal Foch, in his railway carriage in the forest of Compiègne. At 5 a.m. on 11 November, the two sides signed an armistice agreement to come into effect six hours later.

AT 11 AM ON THE 11th day of the 11th month of 1918, the guns of Europe fell silent after more than four years of war. The problems of war were now replaced by the equally pressing problems of peace. Germany had asked for an armistice (cease-fire) in order to discuss a possible peace treaty. She had not surrendered but her soldiers were surrendering in hordes and her navy had mutinied. The Allies wanted to make sure that Germany would never go to war again. The eventual peace treaty re-drew the map of Europe and forced Germany to pay massive damages to the Allies. German armed forces were reduced in size and strength and Germany lost a great deal of land and all of her overseas colonies.

DISPLACED PEOPLE
Many refugees, like these Lithuanians, were displaced during the war. The end of hostilities allowed thousands of refugees – mainly French, Belgians, Italians, and Serbians whose lands had been occupied by the Central Powers – to return home to their newly liberated countries. In addition, there were as many as 6.5 million prisoners of war who needed to be repatriated. This complex task was finally achieved by autumn 1919.

SPREADING THE NEWS
News of the armistice spread around the world in minutes. It was reported in newspapers and typed out in telegrams, while word-of-mouth spread the joyous news to each and every member of the local neighbourhood.

VIVE LA PAIX!
In Paris (below), French, British, and American soldiers joined Parisians in an impromptu procession through the city. In London, women and children danced in the streets while their men prepared to return from the front. In Germany, the news was greeted with a mixture of shock and relief that the fighting was at last over.

SIGNING THE TREATY
These soldiers watching the signing of the Treaty of Versailles had waited a long time for this moment. The Allies first met their German counterparts in January 1919. The Americans wanted a fair and just treaty that guaranteed democracy and freedom to all people, while both France and to a lesser extent Britain wanted to keep Germany weak and divided. Negotiations almost broke down several times before a final agreement was reached in June 1919.

THE TREATY OF VERSAILLES
The peace treaty that ended the war was signed in the Hall of Mirrors in the Palace of Versailles near Paris, on 28 June 1919. Sir William Orpen's painting shows the four Allied leaders watching the German delegates sign the treaty ending German imperial power in Europe, just 48 years after the German Empire had been proclaimed in the same hall.

THE PEACE TREATIES
The Treaty of Versailles was signed by representatives of the Allied powers and Germany. The Allies signed subsequent treaties elsewhere in Paris with Austria in September 1919, Bulgaria in November 1919, Turkey in April 1920, and Hungary in June 1920. By then, a new map of Europe had emerged.

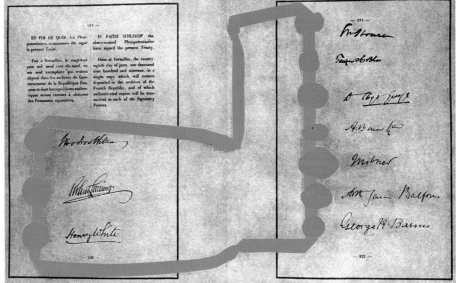

The Treaty of Versailles

General Foch

Georges Clemenceau

David Lloyd George

Vittorio Orlando

Giorgio Sonnino

THE VICTORIOUS ALLIES
The negotiations in Paris were dominated by French premier Georges Clemenceau (supported by General Foch), British premier David Lloyd George, Italian premier Vittorio Orlando – seen here with his foreign minister, Giorgio Sonnino – and the US president Woodrow Wilson. Together the Big Four, as they became known, thrashed out the main details of the peace settlement.

The cost of the war

THE COST OF THE First World War in human lives is unimaginable. More than 65 million men fought, of whom more than half were killed or injured – 8 million killed, 2 million died of illness and disease, 21.2 million wounded, and 7.8 million taken prisoner or missing. In addition, about 6.6 million civilians perished. Among the combatant nations, with the exception of the USA, there was barely a family that had not lost at least one son or brother; some had lost every male member. Entire towns and villages were wiped off the map, and fertile farmland was turned into deadly bogland. Financially, the economies of Europe were ruined, while the USA emerged as a major world power. Not surprisingly, at the end of 1918, people hoped they would never again have to experience the slaughter and destruction they had lived through for the past four years.

ONE LIFE
A soldier stands on Pilckem Ridge during the Battle of Passchendaele in August 1917. The crudely made cross indicates a hastily dug grave, but many soldiers were engulfed by the mud and their graves remained unmarked.

THE UNKNOWN SOLDIER
Many of the dead were so badly disfigured that it was impossible to identify them. Plain crosses mark their graves. Thousands more just disappeared, presumed dead. Both France and Britain ceremoniously buried one unknown warrior – at the Arc de Triomphe, Paris, and Westminster Abbey, London.

AFTERCARE
The war left thousands of soldiers disfigured and disabled. Reconstructive surgery helped repair facial damage, while masks and prosthetics were used to cover horrible disfigurements. Artificial limbs gave many disabled soldiers some mobility. But the horrors of the war remained with many soldiers for the rest of their lives.

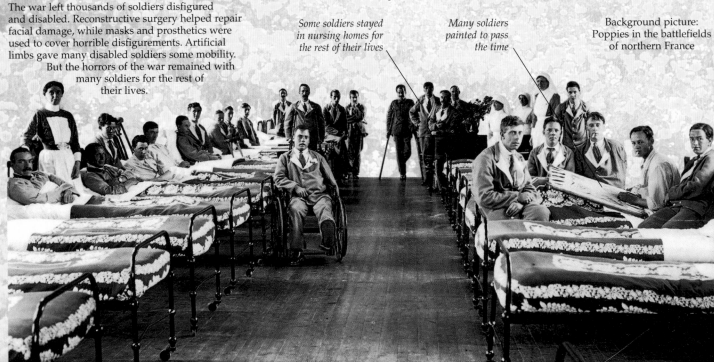

Some soldiers stayed in nursing homes for the rest of their lives

Many soldiers painted to pass the time

Background picture: Poppies in the battlefields of northern France

MEMENTOS

A profusion of flowers, including red Flanders poppies, grew along both sides of the Western Front. Soldiers, such as Private Jack Mudd of the 214 Battalion of the London Regiment (above), would press them as mementos to send home to their loved ones. Mudd sent this poppy to his wife Lizzie before he was killed, in 1917, in the Battle of Passchendaele. Canadian doctor, John McCrae, wrote the poem *In Flanders Fields* after tending wounded soldiers near Ypres in 1915. His mention of poppies in the poem inspired the British Legion to sell paper poppies to raise money for injured soldiers, and as a sign of remembrance for the dead.

WAR MEMORIALS

The entire length of the Western Front is marked with graveyards and memorials to those who lost their lives in the war. At Verdun, the French national mausoleum and ossuary (burial vault) at Douaumont (below) contains the remains of 130,000 unidentified French and German soldiers. There are 410 British cemeteries in the Somme valley alone.

Prussian Iron Cross

Victoria Cross (V.C.)

FOR GALLANTRY

Every combatant nation awarded military and civilian medals to honour bravery. Five million Iron Crosses were given to German soldiers and their allies. Over two million Croix de Guerre were issued to French soldiers, military units, civilians, and towns, and 576 Victoria Crosses, Britain's highest award, were presented to British and Empire troops.

French *Croix de Guerre*

Index

Acknowledgements

Dorling Kindersley and the author would like to thank:
Elizabeth Bowers, Christopher Dowling, Laurie Milner, Mark Pindelski, and the photography archive team at the Imperial War Museum for their invaluable help; Right Section, Kings Own Royal Horse Artillery for firing the gun shown on page 10.
Editorial assistance: Carey Scott
Index: Lynn Bresler

The publishers would also like to thank the following for their kind permission to reproduce their photographs:
a=above, b=below, c=centre, l=left, r=right, t=top

AKG London: 6l, 7crb, 36br, 37bl, 38cl, 38bl, 41tr, 42c, 42bl, 43br, 38cl, 38bl, 41tr, 42c, 42bl, 43br, 52cl, 58–59t, 60c; **Andrew L. Chernack, Springfield, Pennsylvania:** 3tr, 55tr; **Corbis:** 2tr, 6tr, 7tr, 20tr, 22tr, 31tr; Bettmann 8tr, 26–27, 44–45c, 49bl, 55tr, 35bc, 49tl, 54bl, 55t, 55br, 58–59, 61cr; Dave G. Houser 41cr; **Robert Harding Picture Library:** 63c; **Heeres-geschichtliches Museum, Wien:** 8bl; **Hulton Getty:** 14tl, 17tl, 19br, 21br, 33tr, 32–33b, 35clb, 36cra, 41c, 43t, 47cra, 50clb, 51cl, 58tl, 60tl, 60b, 61tr, 61bl; Topical Press Agency 50cl; **Imperial War Museum:** 2tl, 2cr, 8tl, 9bl, 11tr, 10–11t, 12clb, 13cl, 14bc, 15tr, 15cr, 16c, 16b, 17br, 18tr, 18cl, cr, 18br, The Menin Road, 1918, by Paul Nash 19tr, 19cla, 19cr,

19clb, 20bl, 20br, 21tc, 21tr, 22bca, 22bl, 23t, 23br, 24tl, 24c, 26bl, 27tl, 27bc, 26–27b, 28cl, 28cr, 29tr, 29br, 28–29b, 30tr, 30cl, 31br, 32l, 32c, 33tl, 33cr, 35cb, 35bl, 34–35c, 36clb, 37tl, 38tr, 39cr, 39br, 40cl, 40br, 41tl, 41b, 45br, 44–45b, 48cr, 48bl, 50bc, 51tl, 51c, 52bl, 53cr, 53br, 54tl, 56cl, 57tr, 57cr, 56–57b, 56–57c, 58b, 59tr, 59b, The Signing of Peace in the Hall of Mirrors, Versailles, 1919–20, by Sir William Orpen 61tl, 62tl, 62c; **David King Collection:** 46bl, 47tl, 58cla; **National Army Museum:** 44bl; **National Gallery Of Canada, Ottawa:** Transfer from the Canadian War Memorials, Dazzle ships in dry dock at Liverpool, 1921, by Edward Wadsworth 39tl; **Peter Newark's Military Pictures:**

13ac, 42tr; **RAF Museum, Hendon:** 34cla, 34cl; **Roger-Viollet:** 9tr, 9cr, 11br, 13cr, 19tl; Boyer 17bl; **Spink and Son Ltd:** 3tl, 4tr, 43bc; **Telegraph Colour Library:** J.P. Fruchet 62c; **Topham Picturepoint:** 42tl, 46tl, 47br, 46–47b, 62b; ASAP 43cl; **Ullstein Bild:** 8–9c, 46tr.

Jacket credits:
AKG London: back cra, back bl; **Imperial War Museum:** back tl, back br, front tl, front c, front cra, front b (staged image), inside front bl, spine b; **Topham Picturepoint:** front cl.

All other images © Dorling Kindersley.
For further information see:
www.dkimages.com